TWILIGHT VISIONS

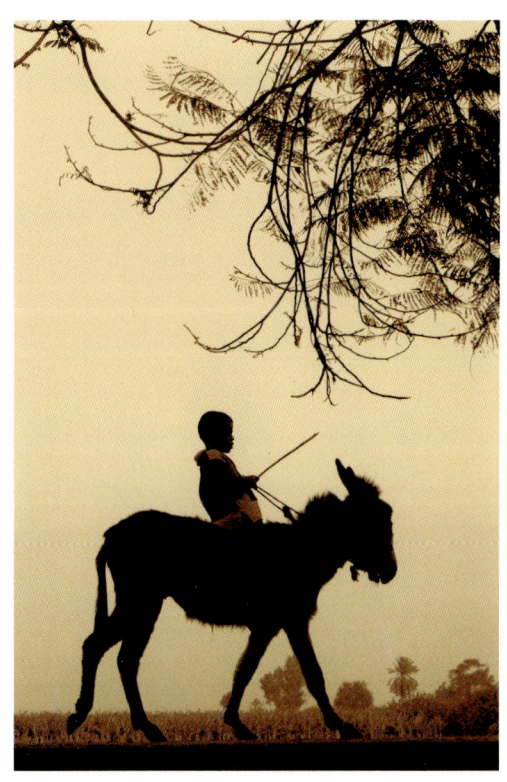

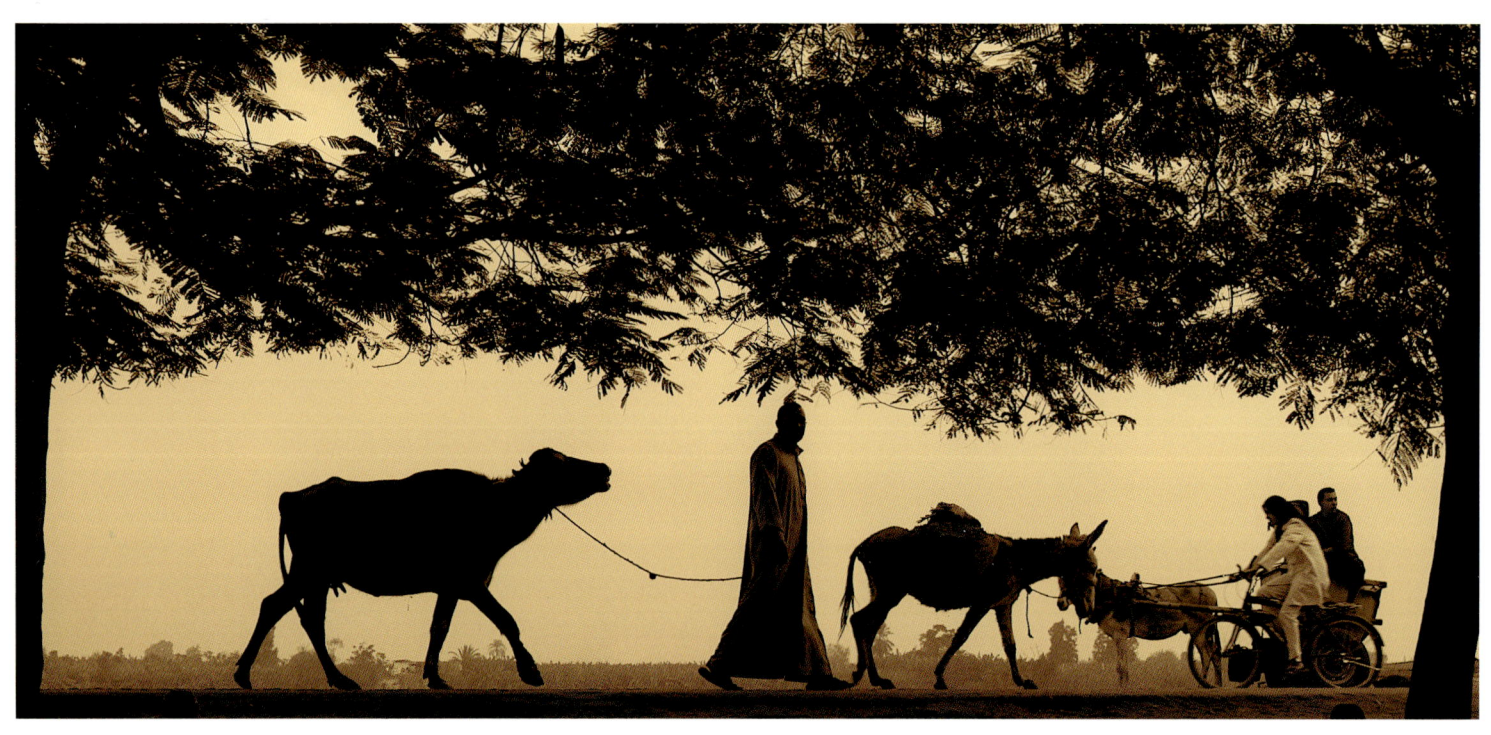

TWILIGHT VISIONS
IN EGYPT'S NILE DELTA

ANN PARKER

Text by Muhammad Afifi Matar

Translated by
Ferial J. Ghazoul

The American University in Cairo Press
Cairo   New York

Copyright © 2008 by
The American University in Cairo Press
113 Sharia Kasr el Aini, Cairo, Egypt
420 Fifth Avenue, New York, NY 10018
www.aucpress.com

Photographs and Introduction copyright © 2008 by Ann Parker

"Early Awakenings" by Muhammad Afifi Matar is extracted from his book *Awa'il ziyarat al-dahsha: Hawamish al-takwin*, second edition, Cairo: General Egyptian Book Organization, 2006. Copyright © Muhammad Afifi Matar. English translation copyright © Ferial J. Ghazoul/*Alif*. Sections 1, 3–11, 13, and 14 appeared as "Wonders of Childhood: On the Margins of Formation," translated by Ferial J. Ghazoul, in *Alif: Journal of Comparative Poetics* 27 (2007): 97–106, © *Alif* 2007.

All rights reserved. No part of this publication may be reproduced, stored in a retrieval system, or transmitted in any form or by any means, electronic, mechanical, photocopying, recording, or otherwise, without the prior written permission of the publisher.

Dar el Kutub No. 4339/08
ISBN 978 977 416 186 5

Dar el Kutub Cataloging-in-Publication Data

Parker, Ann
Twilight Visions: in Egypt's Nile Delta / Ann Parker.—Cairo: The American University in Cairo Press, 2008
p.   cm.
ISBN 977 416 186 6
1. Egypt—description and travel
916.2

1 2 3 4 5 6 7 8   14 13 12 11 10 09 08

Designed by Andrea El-Akshar
Printed in China

CONTENTS

Early Awakenings *by Muhammad Afifi Matar*   vi

Photographer's Introduction   xx

Twilight Visions   1

Acknowledgments   102

Early Awakenings

Muhammad Afifi Matar

1. Motherly Intoning

When my mother used to ask me to repeat what I had memorized of the short suras of the Quran up to the long ones, from the 'Amma section to the Tabarak section, and correct my mistakes with her melodious voice—her face illuminated with joy, her eyes shut—the lofty rhythm would embrace everything with its purity and the world would take the shape of an enthralling rosary of voices and taut harmony.

On the morning of the first day I attended the *kuttab*, a cloud of intertwined rhythms gathered at a distance above the house of Sayyidna, our master. As my steps came closer, the intertwining and resonance of these rhythms increased. The *kuttab* was a large room in the house of Sayyidna. When I took my place on the mat among a group of beginners, I became frightfully and alarmingly aware of Sayyidna's voice as he scolded his wife and young daughter, who were behind the door. Then he raised his hoarse and harsh voice with the verses of the short suras. I said to myself: The Quran must be a woman, and the verses unadulterated motherhood, unknown to men. I realized that everything I had learned from the Quran by heart had dropped out of my memory . . . and I cried.

2. My Grandfather's House

When the wind moves gently or swiftly, the leaves of the reeds ruffle, making a sound resembling the clapping of a child or the whirring of a spindle. Gloomy darkness surrounds the dense reeds, conjuring in the imagination shadowy foxes, snakes, and mice. Behind the reeds, fields stretch out, luminous with verdure and sunlight. My grandfather sits in the courtyard of the house, on a white sheepskin from the sacrificed animal of the Great Feast. He holds in his hand the tail of a white horse, waving it to the right and to the left. Short of stature, he sits straight as a pole; from his cracked teeth, the letter *s* comes out as a cheerful, moist whistle.

My grandfather's tales were about the living and the dead, as they entered and departed, between wedding celebrations and tearful sighs. From these dusty, smoky doors, my grandmother came out from the labors of birth to the sorrows of absence. My mother never saw her, even though she continued to dream of her, until she responded to her last call.

In all his tales, I could not forget the girl Tatar. When she laughed, the sun seemed to peek out from her creases; when she cried, rain fell; and when she smiled, the face of a full moon shone.

My father prompted me once to stand away from the house's threshold and cry out rhythmically:

Abu Ammar
The house is ruined
Because of a nail.

My grandfather exploded in anger and came chasing me. I ran to my father, who laughed uproariously.

The horse's tail fluttered in my grandfather's hand, and scattered words tumbled from his continuous chatter. I never saw him silent. I picked up the threads of a mysterious tale about his passionate love for a woman whom he married after he had had a number of sons and grandsons. In his passion, he squandered all that he owned and only smatterings were left.

As I grew a few years older, I came to understand my father's allusions to the nail and grasped the provocative hint that inflamed my grandfather with anger. I used to joke with my mother and tease her by saying: "Daughter of Shafiqa and Zakiya's man," referring to the two wives I used to see sitting around my grandfather when I visited him, each holding his lit cigarette. My mother used to scold me with tender, motherly anger and repeat to me her saying: "The son is born, the brother is there, but the father is lost," alluding to the fact that her father was dearer to her than a son or a brother.

Whenever I entered or passed by my grandfather's house after his death, I would see the face of beautiful Tatar appearing from the mist of dust and smoke, transfusing what remained of the ruins with its mysterious magic.

3. The First Loyalty
A thin thread of distant kinship attached us. I was proud of him and impressed by his strength. As a family elder, he was commanding, yet tender.

I used to hover around him, fearing his angry eruptions and the attacks of his demented mind. I would contemplate his strong body with its bulging muscles, watch his long, coarse, burly fingers—scales and ridges piling up on their joints—as he folded iron rods and pieces of steel with this hands, and as he rubbed the basalt stones, and broke glass and coins between his fingers. He made bets with people on difficult manly tasks—from gorging himself with great amounts of food to lifting heavy weights, from pushing others around to salvaging bulls and camels fallen into the wells of waterwheels.

His wife was slender and spent—slowed down by her ailment and hardly able to walk. When she passed by and called him in her weak and cracked voice, he rushed to her with eyes bright with joy and the glimmer of childhood. He walked humbly behind her with his head lowered. I said, then, to myself: Whatever your strength and power will be in the coming days, and in the prime of your manhood, do not let go of your command and do not humbly give your loyalty except to the weakest and most fragile of things: a buzzing insect, the weeds of a pond, the egg of a bird, the smell of sweat, or the tear of someone beaten.

4. The Chill of the Soft G
Like a blossom cut off from its tree, I used to sit in front of the ironing shop just after dawn, getting warmed up by the glowing live coals inside the big foot-iron with its sturdy box. I would stretch out my hand and quickly carry the hot glow to the sides of my ice-cold ears. Feet, bare or shod, left their traces on the carpets of sawdust in front of the shop. After warming up the bread my mother had put in my cloth bag, and exactly at 7:30, the ironer would move his glowing brazier into his shop. Through the clear glass, the brazier emitted shattered gold and fluid silver. Then I would run as the bell of the school nearby jingled.

When a tall, fair, blue-eyed boy looked at me and made fun of my shabbiness, and of the country way I pronounce the soft *g*, an icy hand clutched my body and the rips in my ragged clothes opened up to the fingers of icy air.

5. The Poet
In the expanse of the fields, I used to hear them breaking into melodious songs, with what they had memorized of the poet's words. The air would be filled with horses and rattling sabers. The bright serenity in the morning would take its embellishment from the spears, javelins, and battle scenes.

When I saw him for the first time, with his lofty height, elegant turban, and *quftan* flowing with silk, brocade, and rainbows, I thought him a body of music pouring forth words.

I stayed up all night with them until dawn. He was narrating the story of the eagle that had snatched the pearl necklace from the hand of the lover and soared with it toward the seventh heaven, while the lover ran under his shade, screaming and entreating him to return the necklace of his beloved. I panted and began to sweat. After that, whenever I saw a bird circling in the air I would always look between its claws in the hope of seeing the necklace of some lover.

6. Confrontation
Boy's manhood and girl's motherhood begin in our village at the age of seven. With the roughness of early weaning from play and poor man's games, our steps begin to intertwine with the struggle for food and the endeavor of melting in the family's sweaty work.

I had not yet forgotten the horrors of afreets and supernatural djinn when my family entrusted me with the responsibility of standing at the waterwheel circuit to prod the cow with the tip of my stick whenever it stopped. It was a strikingly beautiful moonlit night when I turned suddenly to see a small monkey jumping around, gazing at me with his bright eyes. I let out a loud scream of alarm. When my father dashed toward me, asking what had happened, I was too ashamed to divulge my fear of a small monkey. I said the cow had stepped on my foot with its hoof. My father went back to his place at the water in the irrigation canal.

I told myself: Your father did not see the monkey! So I gazed at the point of the terrifying danger, and went little by little toward it. I discovered that it was nothing but the shadow of the mulberry tree, moved by the night breeze. I felt a deep embarrassment and secret shame whenever I looked at the faces of my family.

7. Heart Rending
I did not know that this book would open up the gate of laments and tears for me, which would open wider with time.

I was illiterate then, and had not yet been enrolled in the *kuttab*, when I found the book on the shelf of my uncle's house. I took it and started turning the pages one by one, wetting my fingers with my saliva and counting in a loud rhythmic voice: That's one, that's two, that's three, . . . Suddenly, a picture appeared under my fingers. I brought it close to my eyes to see its finest details.

The picture was of a little girl with shabby clothes, crying and lamenting under a coffin carried by four men. Her screams broke my heart, and my eyes were wet with tears. A dusty whiff of grief arose from the pages, which I continue to smell. From that distant moment, I have been gathering tears from books. My heart is rent for the cries of the dead and the living.

8. Fearful Beings
To reach the school in the nearby town, my mother used to accompany me every day at dawn to the train station by the light of a tin lamp with a thick wick, while the wind played with its flame.

We walked along the road between the ghost trees. She would tell me, in her persistent chattering, about those who died under the train wheels and how they came out in the dark night to relive their lives. The women came out carrying sacks of grain or flour, the men straddling their riding animals, boys and girls bantering and fooling. She used to say: "If you get scared and run, they will chase you and hurt you incurably. But if your heart is strong, and you recite the Quranic verses you know by heart, they will disappear and go back to their deathbeds in the silence and darkness of the earth."

When my father said that it was not appropriate any more for me to seek protection from my mother, the earth narrowed down on me. The twilight before dawn encircled me with afreets, djinn, and the ghosts of the dead. I was alarmed, and the roads of escape were closed. I said to myself: It is death and no more! In a challenge like suicide, I went out in the darkness before dawn, and I passed intentionally by the places of the hidden dead and the concealed ghosts, by the hiding spots of djinn and afreets.

9. An Apocalyptic Scene
I have known winter in many countries, experienced its air and gale, its storming cold, pouring rain, swift wind. Yet one single winter night—with its fearful events—is engraved in my mind. It came to be the emblem and the indicator of 'winter,' whenever the word occurs in writing or speech.

My father was away on a trip, and we—my mother, my siblings, and myself—were trying to warm ourselves by sitting around the glowing earthenware brazier. As winter beauty chased summer beauty, the clamor of wind and the rattling of thunder started to reach us. The rain falling on the firewood and straw on top of the house sounded like a downpour, rising more and more until raindrops began dripping and seeping inside the house. Water trickled everywhere. As the sky shook with thunder, and the waters flowed under the doors we were alarmed. I remembered what I had heard about Noah's flood, as my mother struggled against the water, scooping it out with all the kitchen pans and kneading pots we had. But the water rose, rendering the floor of the house a mire in which our feet sank.

With a terrified look in her eyes, my mother screamed in the loudest voice: "Abdallah, boy! This is the Day of Judgment!" Images of graves splitting open with their corpses, figures of the dead dragging their shrouds and skeletons, and of the living as they die just before resurrection erupted in my memory. The horror of the scene made me scream and burst into tears: "Mother, are we to die when father is away and alone? How can we be resurrected if he is not with us? Can't we wait a little?"

10. The Escape of the Catfish
I did not know that I was participating in fabricating a lie, which the family had to pay for, without a chance of confessing and showing regret.

Two days had passed since the strange man had been with us. He had a dark face and very bright and wide black eyes, wore threadbare clothes, and his body was manifestly strong. He was working for us in exchange for food, and some money. He was so furtive and silent that he left no opportunity for anyone in the family, or among the neighbors, to ask him about anything that might define his personality.

After having been to the fields at dawn and come back, he asked my father if he could fish in the distant canal, as it had almost run dry, leaving puddles of water full of fish, and asked if I could come with him to see it. My father ordered me to go, and when we reached the distant canal the man said to me: "You will be with me when I fish. If your father asks you, tell him that the canal is almost dry, and the fish are jumping around in the shallow water."

I did not see any fish, and the canal had plenty of water, which made fishing difficult, but my joy in participating in a fishing expedition made me lie and tell my father what the strange man had asked me to say.

The man said that fish were plentiful only in darkness, at night. Daytime proved to be a burden for me, as I was looking forward to the fishing adventure. My mother prepared our supper, and we took it with us. The strange man placed me behind him on the back of the donkey.

He said: "Sit under this tree and do not move, so that I can search for a better place for fishing." I sat waiting, and the wait was long. I was overcome by sleep, and when my father and some neighbors startled me, I woke up scared. They looked for the strange man and the donkey everywhere, but found no traces of them. It was a memorable day in the history of the village.

11. The Circle of Death

I did not see her relax once, for even a moment, from the time my eyes opened upon her and I became part of her world, a heavy burden added to her numerous burdens. In fact, all her burdens were but one burden, which struck her very existence the way tyrants strike without mercy. It was the burden of the sole master and proprietor, the axis of life—when awake and asleep. If she felt sick, he would become fidgety, and he would puff with anger and impatience. He would urge her to get up. All day and night, she would rush like a bee to attend to his desires—which were stated as commands, in an aggressive language charged with condescension and reproach, with exaggerated and extreme modes of criticism and scorn.

The house was never free—day and night—of the smoke circling up from heating the water five times a day in the earthenware jug on the oven over the firewood. Whenever he slept, or went out, or returned, his presence polarized the life of all those in the household—his habits and moods devoured them all. She would have tolerated all this, seeing it as normal, but she could not tolerate or forgive him smothering her children with his cruel blows. Thousands of times she told me about this; her last words as she lay dying was a death sentence of a unique type, a delayed retributive justice.

Her husband had a son from another woman in another distant village, whom he had divorced before he married her. The other woman took her son with her during the nursing and early childhood period. When he was seven, my father went to take him back from his mother, so he would live at home with his younger siblings.

Her husband's son was spoiled by his mother, and puffed with hatred for his father and siblings. This pushed him into rejection and rebellion from the first moments of his entry into our household. He was then stunned by his father's violence, and horrified by his merciless beatings and blows. Thousands of times my mother said that the beatings of my father on his poor son left red and blue marks on her own infant son. She took her husband's son and escaped to her father's house, not only for his protection but also to protect her two older boys. It came to be known by the neighbors as the story of the stepmother who defied the known legacy of stepmothers, by making the protection of her stepson a matter of life and death for herself. But her husband's impetuous tyranny and glowing anger overwhelmed her. Thus she buried her two sons. In twenty years, she handed six male and one female offspring to the grave, and miscarried twice. She was quite sure that the blood of the dead smeared the hands of her husband, and twisted around his neck.

Only two sons and a daughter of hers escaped death. They grew up with their half brother, and they all eventually married. When her husband's son had a baby, an extraordinary vitality possessed her. She took the baby on her lap to take care of him. We were all surprised when her breasts leaked milk at the age of sixty.

Her husband died ten years before her, but she continued to tell the story of her dead children. When she felt her end was approaching, her only request to her children, and to all her relatives, was not to place her with her husband in one grave.

12. The Siftings of Cholera

A rapid fire flared up as the water met the quicklime in the pit, emitting a subdued hiss and sending scorching steam upward. I was then seven years old and I wanted to push my hand into this unusual mix to experience the magical act and the astonishing miracle: a fire out of water and hidden embers in the whiteness of the quicklime that looked like wheat flour.

The grownups sternly rushed to move me away, but all day I watched the lime plaster after its secret fire had been extinguished and it was blended with straw, to be carried by the workers in large bowls and wooden slabs up to the *usta*, the skilled mason on the scaffolding. The *usta* would take some of the mix on his wooden slab and then plaster the walls with it, using a trowel or a float. These were the last touches needed to complete our new house after our old one had become too crowded and derelict. There was only one room left in our old house—with a high vault that ended with a small circular opening from which pale light entered— and a barn without a door; when we raised its floor by putting dry dirt beneath the animals, their urine would dribble across the threshold of the vaulted hall, and we would wake up with the seepage trickling under our mats and wetting our mattresses.

The experience of demolishing and building, of listening to the *mawwal*s chanted by the *maallim* Muhammad Hablas the master mason as he raised the scaffolding course after course were some of the joys rendered by working, constructing, and shaping the house moment by moment. The most profound impression of the experience, which left me astonished and fascinated, was the scene of the quicklime—what an apt name!—when its flames rose, exhaling and hinting at its hidden secret. It was this fascination itself that turned later into angry torment and painful anguish.

The cholera epidemic spread over the country, disseminating a terrifying tension and dark fear, even of the touch of hands, the mouthful of bread, the earthenware jug, the spout of the water jar, or the sip of water. A group of soldiers from the police post came to the village and started turning over baskets of tomatoes, fruit, and vegetables onto the ground and trampling on them with their heavy boots. They confiscated the wares of the poor peddlers: the *taamiya* beancakes, the dishes of *fuul*, and the cartons of sweets.

It was horror beyond which there is no horror, a confused and desperate effort to fight against the agonies of the unknown, the daily tracking of the number of dead the length and breadth of the country, accounts of the containment of death and the good news of vaccination and inoculation. The utmost necessity of using lemon juice on everything raised the price of a lemon to one whole pound, more than an agricultural worker earned in a month. I had never seen my village in such a state of misery and anguish, colored by the dusty yellowness of death, as I did in those days.

A number of villagers fell victim to the epidemic. The first to fall was my cousin Basyuniya. She was in the fever hospital of the main town. We were informed of her death by cholera, but instead of bringing her body to be buried in the family tomb, she was buried in a grave of quicklime there in the town. I was struck by a fierce terror beyond description.

My mind and psyche were filled with what I had heard about the resurrection of the dead for the First Judgment: The dead person's soul returns and he comes alive to face the two angels of death, Munkar and Nakir, as they ask: "Who is your God and who is your prophet and what is your sacred book?" Grasped by fear, the deceased tries to stand up but hits his head on the roof of the grave, and sees the frightening angels. If he is one of those fortunate ones with a firm belief, his heart will not waver and he will have the courage to answer with confidence, eloquently and calmly. His grave becomes then a garden of paradise. But if he is ill-fated, his grave becomes a pit of fire, and he is whipped and clubbed, and devoured by the fangs of the fearless bald one, the immense cosmic python of seventy heads, in each head seventy fangs and seventy tongues to emit poison and tear the flesh. Thus the condemned, lost soul remains in the infernal pit until the Last Judgment.

I began to scream the scream of repressed fear, of the images of death, of the phantasms of the First Judgment, of the horrors of what I knew of the effects of quicklime. What a terrible grave for you, my cousin, and what a washing in flames between your blood, your bones, and the white and frightful shroud of siftings!

13. The Flood Scene

He stood among us with his short-sleeved, open shirt. His hair was pitch black and cut short, army-style. His complexion was dark and luminous. His eyes were somewhat bulging; he had gapped teeth, and youthful vitality. He used to take pleasure in articulating words, and narrating historical information in a clever and appealing way.

He was only a few years older than we were, and seemed as if he were one of us. We used to listen, captivated, to his discourse on the European Renaissance. Occasionally, he would surprise us with a display of fascinating prints and copies of the works of Leonardo da Vinci, Michelangelo, and Raphael. It was the first time I had seen the genius of colors, art, and design, and come to know the motifs of painting and sculpture. I grasped their relation to the Renaissance and Humanism, and the emergence of literature and art inspired by the Classical period and its esthetic values and intellectual achievements.

I cannot now reproduce the exquisite pleasure that overtook me and made me tremble, moistening my eyes, as I examined the richness of the paintings in the Sistine Chapel—Genesis, the Fall, the Flood, the biblical narratives of the prophets, the struggle between good and evil, and the universe of angels and saints. I almost cried as I followed the details of the Flood. My eyes were fixed on a woman carrying her infant as her son held onto her leg. The painting was so bound up with fear and horrified anxiety, with the touch of wet storms, and the explosion of earth and sky with water.

The history teacher in the mid-1950s in the secondary school of Menouf became one of my spiritual heroes, a cultural pioneer who opened for me the gates of profound excitement and exhausting search for the universe of the plastic arts, with their varied ages, schools, and artists.

I used to wait for him every morning in front of the school gate. He was one of a galaxy of teachers who would come each morning from Cairo, and other cities and towns, by train. I never had a conversation with him. How could someone like me address the history of humanity with its art, literature, and epics as embodied in a man?

In the mid-year exam, I wrote in my answer a comment on the lack of precision in one of the questions. I thought that the depth of our silent relationship had created a space in which I could join him in a dialog. I thought he would be delighted with my comment.

The next day, he called with anger: "Who is so-and-so?" I stood up anxiously. He said: "You are impertinent." And before he could go on, he was shocked to see me break into silent tears. He said: "What is wrong with you?" I said: "Any teacher but you. You in particular." He asked me to clarify. I asked him with tears in my eyes: "Don't you know how much I respect you and admire you?" His eyes were wide with surprise and he asked me to sit down.

Just before the end of the school year he disappeared for good, and we did not hear of him anymore. I found out that he had been transferred to another city—Cairo or Benha—and I felt horribly orphaned, and estranged. I was particularly upset because I knew neither his full name nor his address, as I had never dared to ask. Thus he disappeared in the darkness of the unknown. But his face and his voice remained a beacon for me. Whenever I entered a museum, or an art exhibition, or turned the pages of an art book anywhere in the world, his face and voice would come back to me. I have asked thousands of times: Who are you, Sir? What is your name? And where are you now?

More than thirty years later, when I was crossing Ramses Square with members of my family, I saw him talking to someone in the distance. It was him; nothing had changed in him except a few gray hairs, and a light plumpness. He had the same elegance and grand, inspiring presence. His gapped teeth were the same, and so were his shining eyes. Both he and I turned around, gazing at each other in recognition and with cautious recall. I said to those with me, "Wait for me," and I dashed to him with joyful excitement. I was about to catch up with him when the crowded square separated him from me. I began to run like a madman, staring at faces, but his own face had disappeared. When my eyes became wet with tears, I saw the square as if it were a scene from the painting of the Flood.

14. The Son of Two Mothers

It was as if I were the axis of a hand mill, around which a deadly stone moved to grind my siblings, one by one: three brothers died before I was born; another three brothers and a sister died after I was born. I stood between these two waves, rocked by stormy death. I lived with the stories of the ones that passed away before me, and I gulped down the sorrows of those who were snatched by death from my own arms.

My mother fought valiantly to break away from this death curse, to have me avoid the ruthless fate, and save me from the ravishes of the uneven struggle between her and the tribes of djinn and ghosts. She undertook fierce battles in my defense, starting with the twilight of dawn. She took me by the hand, holding a stripped palm leaf in the other hand, and—in a tradition well established in the practice of professional beggars—she passed by seven doors of households, all owned by someone called Muhammad. In a voice that melted hearts with sorrow and provoked pity and mercy, she asked for alms from each household for the poor boy Abdallah. It had been determined that each offering would be a hollowed silver coin and a flat loaf of bread. Thus she collected the hollowed silver coins and seven flat loaves of bread. We returned home before sunrise. The flat loaves were my food for seven days, and as for the coins she asked a blacksmith to turn them into an anklet that she put around my right foot, warning me that I should never take it off, no matter what.

At sunset one day, my mother took me to a woman in the village who would 'buy' me, and adopt me so that I would become her son through purchase and adoption. They had already arranged this, and the horrific ritual began.

The other woman passed me through the neck of her wide gallabiya and out through its wide hem seven times. I cried out as I slid over her naked body. Then my mother firmly said: "This is your mother; you had been deposited as a trust with me, and now I am returning you to her."

She left me and went out, while I cried out and hung onto her clothes. The other woman held me tight, and tried to keep me in her household. She began cosseting and cuddling me in her arms. She offered me a feast of eggs, cheese, and yogurt sweetened with sugar, as I gazed curiously at what was around me in the house.

She pointed to a boy about my age and said: "This is your brother Mitwally. You will play and sleep together, and together you will hit anyone who attacks either of you."

The night passed, as I turned over and cried, trying to understand and believe, trying to implant the sentiment of belonging to this new house. I asked myself: Who is my father then?

When the sun rose, the woman told me: "Go to your other mother. From now on, you are the son of both of us. If she angers you, or if you want to play with Mitwally, or eat or spend the night here, don't hesitate."

Thus I became born of two mothers. They shared my love, and overshadowed my early childhood with their warmth and overflowing tenderness. I did not hesitate to move from one to the other. As I grew older, and had escaped the scythe of death, my mother fully explained the act and its meaning. But I continued to feel deeply that I am the child of two women, with a double existence, and I doubly succumbed to the tragedy of their deaths.

15. On the Threshold of Adolescence

We would be engrossed in playing with mud, reeds, date pits, and bottle caps until the sun approached the yellowish twilight. Just before this atelier of creative youth was about to break up, the fresh, beautiful girl surprised us with what she had made. We saw a doll of mud in her hand; we looked at it, dazzled. We were envious, and each of us had a mad impulse to own this extraordinary treasure or to break it so that no one would take hold of it or possess it.

The fresh, beautiful girl had made the features of the mud doll almost alive. She had smoothed it gently and delicately with her saliva until it looked sparkling. She had decorated the breasts and the navel with designs like those on traditional cookies—rounded in gentle and evocative curves. She had decorated the hands with what looked like traces of henna. Between the lips she had planted a few grains of rice, making the doll look as if she were about to smile.

Some years later, in the flight of a magnificent dream, the mud doll appeared from the depth of sleep, having acquired flesh and blood. Before I could voice my astonishment, the henna motifs of flowers and birds fell from her hands and covered our naked bodies.

It was a fleeting moment. I woke up feverish with the ecstasy of discovery and the heaviness of the secret. Frightened, I rushed to bury my clothes, with their indicative traces, under the heap of dirty clothes. I went out with a tremendous sensation that was a mixture of shame, obscure questions, and bold discovery. I went out another person.

Photographer's Introduction

It all started by chance with a late afternoon visit to the home of the *omda*, or mayor, of a typical village in the Egyptian Delta. This century-old dwelling with its tall windows and carved double front doors is in the mud-brick style. Like the village, it reflects both the past and the present. To reach the sitting area at the entrance, visitors climb down a gentle dusty slope, as the house is situated some five meters back from, and a meter and a half below, a narrow but paved road. It is exactly this situation that gives the unique view of a variety of happenings along this road. I realized the first time I visited that these daily comings and goings told a truthful visual tale of a time and a place. I made the decision to document only what I saw on the road, and not to include photographs of daily life in the maze of narrow lanes that make up much of this community. You will not find records of weekly markets, children in school, shopkeepers, or women baking bread. My intention was to concentrate only on the road before me. This self-imposed limitation felt neither restrictive nor contrived, but actually gave me the precise imagery I sought.

From the very first day I sat in front of this old-style home and watched the telling procession pass by, I had the continuing illusion of experiencing a theatrical performance. Because of the slight difference in elevation between the house entrance and the road, the characters in this rural drama appear silhouetted, like shadow puppets, against the sky. What I observed passing back and forth was the essence of traditional Egyptian rural life, sometimes seeming centuries old, sometimes appearing modern. Even that first day, the richness of the imagery entranced me. However, at that time, I had little idea how deeply involved I would become in documenting the happenings on this tiny patch of road bounded by two graceful trees.

I have been photographing rural Egypt for over twenty years, but until I came to visit the *omda* I had never found such a simple but dramatic way to record the essence of fellaheen life. One problem I had battled with was how much I disrupted any space I entered. In towns and villages, children would inevitably spot me from a distance and rush to crowd around me. Within moments I became the focal point, and any semblance of what I had seen and wished to record was shattered. In the many other countries where I had worked, I had rarely caused such a stir.

I kept searching for a way to be less visible, and I found it by chance at the mayor's house. In this unique situation, in spite of the fact that foreigners rarely came to this community, I was virtually ignored. There were several reasons for this apparent anonymity. Partly it was because I was seated in the shadow of the house and out of the normal line of vision. People were also naturally preoccupied by their own activities on the road and, as I returned time and time again, passersby became accustomed to my visits. But the principal underlying reason was that my Egyptian husband and I were always there together and we were the guests of the village *omda*. Those who did notice me from the road saw me interacting with and apparently accepted by a well respected member of the community. Whatever the combination of reasons, during the two years it took to make this book, not one person ever objected to my image-making or even questioned me about it. With this welcome cloak of invisibility, I was left blissfully free to concentrate completely on the quiet dramas that passed before me without affecting them in any way. As I came to know the passing traffic, it became clear that my images represented much more than what was happening in this one village. What I saw was repeated numerous times each day throughout the rich agricultural lands of Egypt's Nile Delta and, with some regional differences, wherever there was arable land in Egypt.

I took my first photograph on 21 October 2005 and the last on 27 October 2007. By that time, I already had more than enough material for a book, a limited edition portfolio, and exhibitions. For each photographic session I positioned myself in the same place, at the outer edge of a concrete slab that defined the gathering area in front of the old house. As soon as I arrived, a traditional wooden bench with a slatted back and arm rests would be turned to face the road. Within minutes, a cup of welcoming tea would be offered. It was as though I was seated front row center looking up at a stage. I was reminded of far-off times, when in London as a small child I would be taken as a very special treat to the theater to see the pantomimes. Instead of treasured opera glasses, a camera now rested in my lap, always ready to be raised.

❖

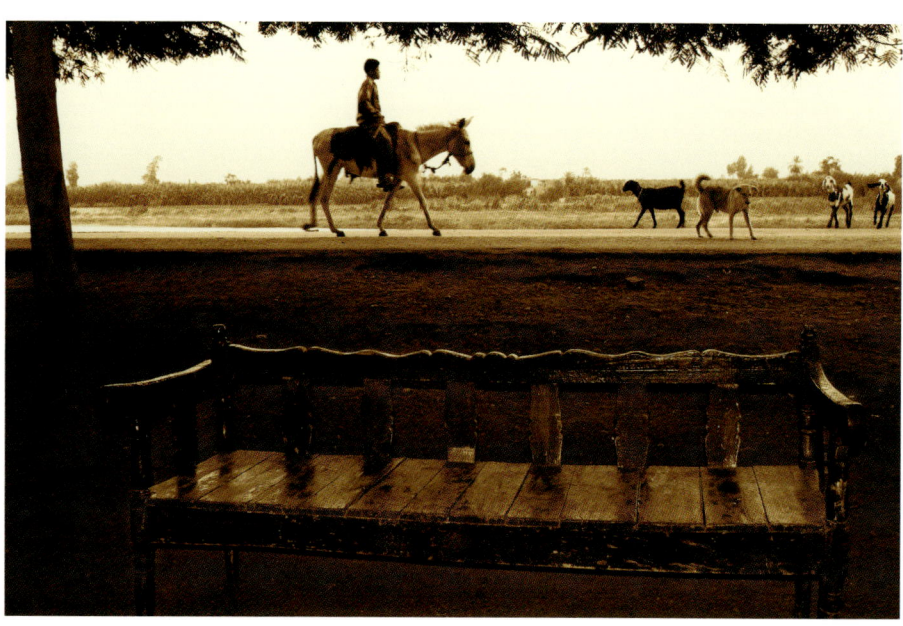

Importantly, the road that passes the *omda*'s house both provides access to the surrounding farmland and links the community to the world beyond. It is not a street lined with bright window displays and eager shoppers typical of more urban communities. Nor is it a highway heavily traveled by the oversized trucks and buses that have come to dominate the network of main roads throughout the Delta. From time to time large vehicles, usually bringing building supplies, do squeeze their way through the village, but they are the exceptions rather than the rule, intrusions that break the timeless mood. Their sheer bulk seems totally out of scale, whereas cars, vans, pickups, and even tractors have slowly nudged their way into the daily life, to become natural to the character of this community.

As the *omda*'s house is situated about halfway through the village, those who pass come almost equally from both directions, depending on the time of day. The 'stage' directly in front of the house is naturally framed on two sides and top and bottom, and all my photographs are taken within this frame. The trunks of two striking flamboyant trees rooted at the edge of the road provide left and right entrances, while the road itself is what I consider the stage floor. This framing is completed by the overhead tree branches. Although bare and lacy in winter and spring, the branches sprout distinctive green leaves for much of the rest of the year, suggesting the fringed drapes that one sees in old theaters (ii). Laden with beautiful red blossoms in early summer, the main branches arch gracefully toward each other, intertwining to form a thick natural canopy that gives the sitting area both dappled shade and an unusual degree of privacy. They also hide the telltale electric and telephone wires that so dramatically changed village life within the memory of the elders of the community. The lower branches of these handsome trees are always kept evenly trimmed to a neat fringe not by clippers but rather by vigilant neighborhood goats. While standing tall on their hind legs, they either frantically wave their front legs to and fro for balance, or support themselves on the sturdy tree trunks. Stretching their necks in a giraffe-like manner, they then proceed to nibble clean any succulent leaves they can reach (48).

Along with dancing goats, chickens of all sizes range freely in front of the house, scratching and pecking the embankment void of any vegetation. Both goats and chickens have a particular liking for the trees' early summer blossoms, which, with the slightest breeze, fall silently to the dusty slope like vermilion snowflakes. These sweet gifts hardly reach the ground before being gobbled up. The goats, always watchful, greedy, and resolute, will butt each other while sounding an aggressive half sneeze to win any prize, but feisty *baladi* chickens are sometimes even swifter.

Throughout the scorching, rainless days of summer, the slope may be dampened from time to time to keep the dust down. On chilly winter evenings, before the family retreats inside, the sitting area is warmed by a brazier fed by corn cobs, small scraps of wood, dried dung patties and other byproducts of farming life. The flickering orange flames from similar cheerful fires are found in the early evening along roadways all across the Delta. They not only give off welcoming heat but are also used for brewing tea and providing small pieces of charcoal for the ever popular *shisha*.

During the midday hours of harsh sunlight there is not much activity on the road, but in the early morning and before dusk it becomes alive with village life. Of the two, the 'coming home' performance is by far the more interesting. The activity begins slowly and lasts for around three hours in the spring, summer, and fall, but much less in the colder winter months. In all seasons, the late afternoon light is consistently perfect for the silhouette clarity I am seeking. By this time, although sunlight still brightens the horizon, the road and its passing traffic are already in the shadow cast by the old house.

In the ever softening light, passersby coming from opposite directions choose their way like schools of fish converging, often pausing to exchange quiet greetings or tell of some recent happening before continuing on their journey (25). In all seasons, donkeys, bicycles, wagons, and even women with torsos as straight as tree trunks and looking like ambulatory bushes come from the fields piled high with fragrant, freshly cut alfalfa to feed the animals before they sleep (72, 83). Milk, butter, and cheeses are said to be much more delicious in the wintertime when the cows and water buffalo are allowed to lie about and have time to eat plentiful amounts of nutritious greens.

After the corn is harvested, leftover stalks are cut and loaded onto any available means of conveyance (33).

These useful leftovers make the quick hot fires needed to warm traditional mud-brick ovens on bread-baking days. Very little goes to waste in this economy. Even animal dung is either used for manure or mixed with straw to make large round patties, which are then dried in the summer sun and usually stored on rooftops to be used for winter fuel. Although life is much easier than it would have been fifty years ago, it still takes a lot of hard work to make ends meet. As some crops, such as wheat, must be harvested as soon as they are mature, farmers will come home for a quick meal after a long day and then head back to the fields, often working cooperatively far into the night. After the grain is separated and winnowed, it is sacked and taken to the mill. The chaff is also ground and stuffed into oversized sacks that are then loaded onto trucks, wagons, and occasionally even camels to become an ingredient in a nourishing fodder (45). At the height of the harvest young women can also be seen dotting the fields like rows of colorful scarecrows, bagging potatoes, sorting onions, and bundling garlic, leaving the men to attend to the heavier work.

❖

Throughout the late afternoon and into the evening, little children stride and scamper back and forth along the road with surprising independence (19, 99). Toddlers too small to keep up with their mothers are hoisted astride one shoulder in the traditionally Egyptian manner (35). Adolescent boys prefer to travel in groups, seemingly very busy but merely out to be seen. Older men take this time of day to take care of errands, go to the mosque, or visit friends (92, 93). Women and girls cross the stage both alone and in chattering clusters (61, 64). Many balance a surprising variety of items on their heads with a dancer-like grace, a skill learned by practicing from a very young age (68, 69). Before electricity, they sometimes even placed lighted kerosene lamps on their heads after dark, leaving their hands free to do evening chores. As most of the houses were in the low-ceilinged mud-brick style, and flammable crops were commonly stored inside or on the roof, numerous fires were caused by this practice.

Beasts of burden—water buffalo, cattle, and an array of horse- or donkey-drawn wagons—are an intrinsic part of the village traffic (7, 15, 87, 97). These may be ridden or driven by men and women of all ages.

Scruffy little donkeys can sometimes be seen pulling small, two-wheeled carts with sizable buckets swinging below. These strangely shaped metal vehicles with rounded bottoms are made specifically to carry off the contents of septic tanks, a stinking reminder of the practicalities of life (22). Far more welcome is a colorful horse-drawn wagon, usually seen in the summer months, set up with several eccentrically shaped containers filled with refreshing tamarind and coconut drinks. The driver moves slowly, clapping his hands to entice customers, particularly children, to buy delicious, cold thirst-quenchers for 25 piastres. His hand movements suggest a greeting to God, which appropriately relates to the Quranic quote on the wagon's side panel: "Their Lord will slake their thirst with a pure drink" (10). As twilight approaches, goats, fat-tailed sheep, ducks, and geese, often teased by feisty dogs, join the evening free-range promenade before being herded into shelters for the night (18, 82, 95).

Sporadically, tractors and other large motorized farm equipment break the quiet mood of the road (9, 23), as do motorcycles and motorbike taxis with vintage-looking sidecars (46, 52, 60). These odd, inexpensive taxis speed villagers to and from the main road a few kilometers away, where passengers disembark to shop, visit family and friends, take care of business, or catch buses to a variety of destinations. Although this side-car appears to have been originally designed to carry a single seated person, more frequently two, three, or even four will find ways to climb aboard and surround themselves with baggage. Minivan buses suffer even more from overload stress, belching noxious fumes in seeming revenge. Many are reaching their last stop in the village and have already disgorged most of their passengers (81).

Particularly on Thursday evenings throughout the summer, honking pickups will pass jammed with celebrants, the men enthusiastically drumming, the women ululating and rhythmically clapping, for this is the most popular night for weddings (77). Marriage parties as well as the preceding engagement gatherings, bride's furniture–delivering processions, and henna celebrations are the brief highlights of a *baladi* girl's life as well as major social events in the village. For her wedding day the bride will be dressed like a queen and often arrive at the celebration in a decorated wedding car. Her hair will be intricately coiffed, and her eyes heavily made up.

Her mask-like face will have taken on a pale doll-like appearance. After slipping into a lavish rented gown, she will stop at a photo studio with her husband and close family members to be recorded in her grandeur. These highly stylized portraits, as well as lengthy videos, will become treasured mementos. Wedding parties, which start around dark and go on into the wee hours, are typically held in the street outside the girl's family house in an area gaily decorated for the occasion. The bride and groom sit like mannequins and individually greet throngs of guests from two large upholstered chairs in the middle of a constructed stage. A jewel box with the bride's collection of gold jewelry may be passed through the crowd to be admired and carefully assessed by the women. Music, either live or canned and usually in a typical disk-jockey style, blares from a sound system. From time to time quite specific announcements are made about monetary gifts.

In stark contrast to boisterous wedding parties are the silent funeral processions, where all-male mourners solemnly walk behind the pall bearers on their way to the cemetery. Women, even when the deceased is female, never join these processions, but gather to mourn at the family home. For men, it is a communal duty to attend these sad functions if at all possible, whether the deceased was a friend or a mere acquaintance.

The most common vehicles passing along the road are the distinctively shaped bicycles seemingly of a former age. The riders become the vehicular chorus dancers in this village drama as they silently weave in and out of traffic or calmly peddle by one by one, appearing to be lost in private thoughts (3). Bicycles of this type cost around 200 Egyptian pounds, or about a quarter the average price of a young donkey, and far less than a motorcycle. They need no feeding, require minimal maintenance, take up little space, and can navigate through narrow alleys, as well as being far faster than walking. Males and females alike depend on bicycles. Schoolgirls peddle their own bikes, while older women usually ride "side saddle" behind men or younger women (50, 89). Even toddlers are given rides, either in baskets or perched directly on the handlebars (51). Little children learn coordination by frantically pedaling bicycles and tricycles scaled to their size (20), whereas teenage boys enjoy riding three and four to a bike, flamboyantly showing off their balancing skills (37). From time to time the community watchman methodically peddles by, making his rounds, easily identifiable by the rifle he casually slings over his shoulder (50).

❖

Along with all these sights, a variety of sounds add another dimension to the the village drama. With motorized traffic, quietness may suddenly be shattered by the piercing of horns, and the unnerving screeching of brakes. In response, both animals and people reluctantly scurry toward the side of the road, but only as much as needed until these intrusions pass. Pedestrians often seem to expect to be given the right of way, ignoring the possibility of accidents. Occasionally, blaring loudspeakers attached to slow-moving pickup trucks or horse-drawn wagons announce in singsong chants that they buy scrap metal, or can exchange full cooking gas canisters for empties. Vehicles loaded with colorful woven floor mats in a pleasing range of patterns, or plastic buckets, bowls, and other household goods, always find buyers for their wares. Other wagons offer large hand-thrown clay *ballas*, reminiscent of amphorae depicted in ancient tomb paintings. These are sold filled with ever-popular strong but delicious molasses, loosely sealed with bunches of corn leaves to keep away the ants and bees. Scratchy voices, blaring music, and rhythmic tapping can be heard long before these markets on wheels become visible, giving people with a few pounds to spare time to come out of their houses and take advantage of a buying opportunity.

Far more bucolic is the metallic clip-clop of horses or the distinctive delicate rhythmic tap of soft-stepping unshod donkeys. These sounds may be further enriched by tinkling bells of various pitches. Even the occasional camel may pass on silent, oversized, padded feet, complaining about his lot in the world with low belching utterances. A muzzle usually hangs from his harness—ready, if needed, to prevent unwelcome bites. In the Delta the camel has lost its former importance as a beast of burden, unlike in Upper Egypt.

Added to these street noises, the ubiquitous calls to evening prayer from several nearby minarets intermingle high above the rooftops in the realm of countless darting and swooping mosque swallows. These incantations not only add balance to the village day, but also connect this community to the rest of Egypt and, more abstractly, to the entire Muslim world. Elegantly delivered Quranic readings may resound from some nearby condolence tent, where the men of the village come to honor a departed villager at the time of the funeral and for the four following Thursdays. Loud or soft, each sound becomes part of the chorus of the road.

❖

In spring, summer, and fall, from mid-afternoon on, the *omda* can almost always be found relaxing on a wooden bench in front of his house. Particularly on hot summer evenings, his wife loves to join him outside, enjoying the status that age has brought her. Both are respectfully greeted by passersby. Some merely wave or nod (92), while others climb down the gentle slope with brief queries or bits of news. A few with more serious business, or friends and family, will sit to be refreshed with small glasses of strong sweet tea and cool clay jugs of water. The giving and taking of cigarettes is one of the commonest forms of camaraderie offered by male visitors. Conversations tend to be hushed, but from time to time loud laughter and hand smacking indicate that a good joke or a pertinent observation has been shared. Discussions frequently turn to the subject of money: what crop is bringing a good or bad price, who has inherited property, or the never-ending rises in the costs of almost everything. Recent funerals and upcoming marriages are also popular topics, as well as plenty of gossip, the lifeblood of rural chatter the world over.

Three generations share this house, and the crisscrossing of family activities weaves the day together. The women come and go carrying food, water, laundry, stacks of aluminum pots and pans, floor mats, and other articles to be washed. Although many houses have running water, the Nile and its vast system of irrigation canals are still frequently used for these chores either to conserve home septic systems or because older houses may not have these amenities. Childcare, time-consuming meal preparations, house cleaning, and other daily work leave little leisure time for the women of the house. Although the *omda's* wife oversees the household chores, much of the actual work traditionally falls to her son's wife, who, according to custom, came to live in the house after marriage. Sometimes younger women members of the family will take a break and sit for a few minutes with friends and relatives. However, as they have more evening chores than the men, these moments of relaxation are by necessity brief.

The outdoor sitting area is much more integrated than within the house, where men and women divide into separate groups and spaces. Small children pause on their way in and out of the house looking for a lap to climb on, to be briefly greeted and teased. They munch on snacks, and may be sent on simple errands. There always seems to be a baby grandchild to be cuddled and passed around. During the school year, older children come from play quite early and go indoors to do homework or, in the case of girls, also to help the women. A small television set is often turned on in the central room of the house, in time for the ever popular serials. These intense melodramas tend to attract women and children more than men, who prefer to chat outside and maybe smoke *shisha*. By dusk, grown sons usually arrive back from the fields, feed and put the animals down for the night, then wash up, eat their own evening meal, and come outside to relax.

As shadows lengthen, the traffic coming from the direction of the farmland has steadily gained momentum and the road is at its busiest, until the sudden curtain of night brings a denouement to the drama. In summertime, both adults and children of all ages stay up late, but in winter the mood is different and doors close early against the chilly evening air. Those who have pressing reasons to be out pass by hurriedly, bundled up with scarf-wrapped faces. Damp cold, like scorching heat, is an enemy to be avoided.

❖

This village, unlike bustling towns or cities along the main roads, has few public diversions. Although there are no big restaurants to sit in, there are several places to buy *fuul*, *taamiya*, and *kushari*. Coffee shops, frequented only by males, provide settings for games of backgammon and dominos, and often a television, usually tuned to a sports channel. Even the occasional billiard table can be found, though this diversion comes with a small but discouraging fee.

Although traditional flat bread is prepared in large quantities once or twice a week at home, bakeries do a brisk business. There are two kinds: those for *aysh baladi*, made from government-subsidized wholewheat flour, and those for white flat bread, rolls, buns, and a small selection of surprisingly plain traditional cookies.

There are also many small shops scattered throughout the village that stock cooking oil, flour, rice, tea, sugar, and other daily necessities. However, fresh produce is typically grown on family land or bought at a big weekly market, when scores of vendors come from outside the village to set up stalls. The fruits and vegetables sold at these markets depend entirely on what is in season. Within the community there are several butchers who can sometimes be seen leading an animal around the village to show what fine meat will be available the following day (6). There are barbers who sometimes still make home calls, beauty salons, tailors, yard goods stores, clothing shops, cobblers, and a photo studio for both small identity-type pictures and lavish wedding portraits. Because gold jewelry is such a status symbol, and a woman's wealth is often tied up in her gold, there is also a jeweler selling bangles, rings, and necklaces in the most popular styles. To this list add lawyers, doctors, and several pharmacies that stay open late. Indeed, most everyday needs can be accommodated in this community of over ten thousand inhabitants, but selections are far more varied and the lights much brighter in nearby towns.

❖

My image-making comes about in a very non-intrusive way. I raise my camera from time to time, but mostly it rests in my lap. I am always waiting for what the famous French photographer Henri Cartier-Bresson called "the decisive moment." There is that split second where everything comes together, and then the moment passes. It is above all about gesture, and silhouetted figures show this with an exaggerated, unencumbered clarity. Over the past two years I have come to know every branch of the twin trees that define my imaginary stage, and can sense how long it will take for an interesting grouping to be precisely in the ideal spot to record (73). But, at the same time, it is the unpredictable that brings the magic. It can be as simple as a sudden hand movement or the tilt of a head (1, 67). As the players in this drama come from both directions, I need to be ever watchful for interrelationships that may or may not unfold. Much of my time is spent looking up and down the road, gauging what might happen. It is a quest, and like all good quests, it holds my interest.

From the beginning, I made the significant choice not to identify the location of this village, both out of consideration for the inhabitants and for esthetic reasons. I deeply respect the privacy of the people I have photographed and also the larger tight-knit community that is their home. During the two years that I sat at the *omda*'s, I remained as unobtrusive as possible. The community, in turn, accepted my presence, but we had very little contact. Unless someone came to sit with the family, we never conversed. Not once did anyone either ask what I was doing or object to my raising my camera.

The silhouette is not only a powerful way of imaging but also provides a degree of anonymity. My intent was not to take specific portraits, but rather to find in fleeting moments an essence of a particular way of life. Neither did I plan to speak of a specific place, but rather of a region. This same lifestyle, and, indeed, similar images could be found in rural communities throughout the Nile Delta. It is also important to note that I neither posed anyone nor coaxed them to pass across my stage. I am not a director, I am a documenter.

I worked with only one lens, resisting shooting with telephoto equipment, a choice made primarily to achieve a visual consistency, but also out of an awareness that large lenses can be intimidating. Although the range of manipulation possibilities is hard to resist with digital printing, none of these images have been changed except to clean up 'noise,' as one would dust a negative. Nothing is added or subtracted except by cropping. I chose to print in sepia because black-and-white seemed too harsh, and color was too distracting. Sepia also perfectly matched the timeless mood I wanted to convey. I have always been a very 'straight' printer in a wet darkroom and have carried this philosophy into the rich but often bewildering new world of digital imaging. I see with an underlying formality, and photograph with deep respect. If one is not very careful, photography can be an incredibly rude art. My aim is to share in a revealing manner a side of Egypt that very few foreigners will have a chance to know, and to document a way of life that is rapidly changing.

❖

Outsiders usually see the Delta from a bus, train, or car on the way between Cairo and Alexandria and the Mediterranean Coast. Although staggering numbers of families head to the beaches along the Mediterranean each summer, few stop along the way for anything but a quick meal at modern convenient rest stops. Except for business, urban Egyptians seldom see any reason to spend time in the Delta. The exception to this rule would be those with village roots or landowners with old family homes and family ties.

There are two main roads north. The 'desert road' is the one more traveled by private cars and lies just west of the Delta. The other choice is known as the 'agricultural road,' which passes directly through the Delta. Both names have become misnomers, as land along the desert road is rapidly being developed for agriculture, and the agricultural road has become more industrialized. Like many major transportation highways throughout the world, much of this route is a visual nightmare of industrial sprawl. Large towns and cities seem to be devouring the rich farmland, in spite of laws forbidding construction on agricultural land. In many areas the air is heavy with pollution and the road is jammed with large trucks.

The express trains from Cairo to Alexandria do pass through some interesting rural scenery, but too fast to catch much of the flavor, leaving an overall impression of flatness and dozens of sprawling towns and cities that most travelers have never heard of. The real character of a traditional life that still flourishes in the Delta is virtually unknown.

❖

I was away from Egypt for six weeks in the fall of 2007 and often thought of my visits to the village. I arrived home and couldn't wait to get back to the *omda*'s house in search of new 'Twilight Visions.' Late the following afternoon, I seated myself as usual and was sipping tea when the full moon rose to greet me. A feeling of happiness came over me. Soon after, two young women walked between the trees that defined my stage (101). As I raised my camera I realized how much I had missed this special place. I also knew it was time to make a book.

TWILIGHT VISIONS

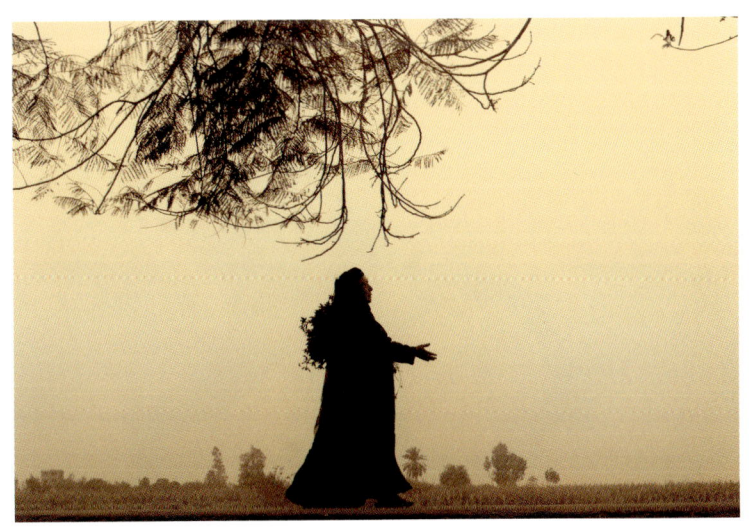

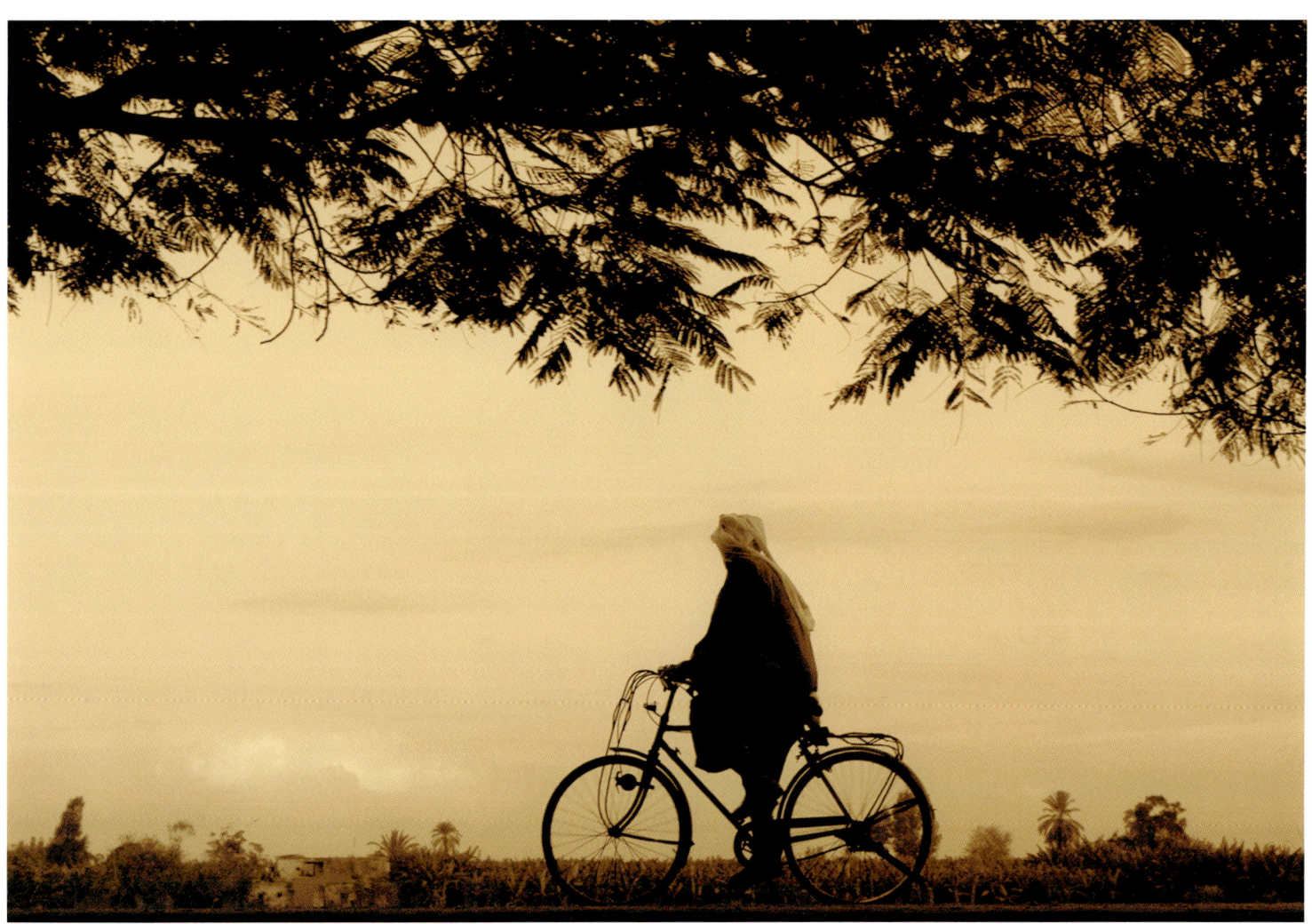

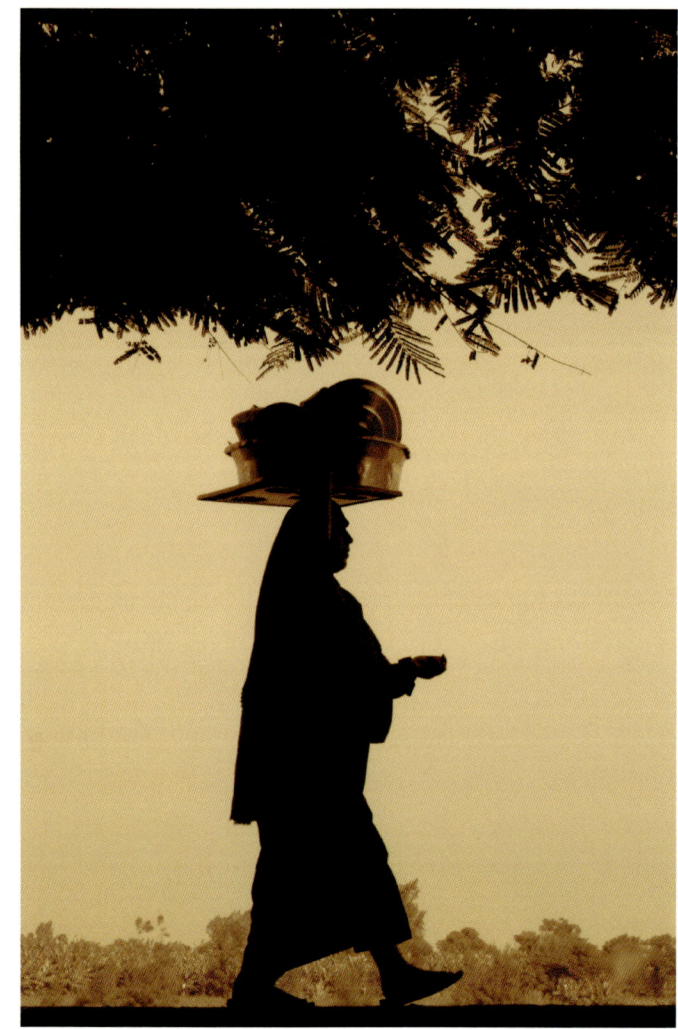

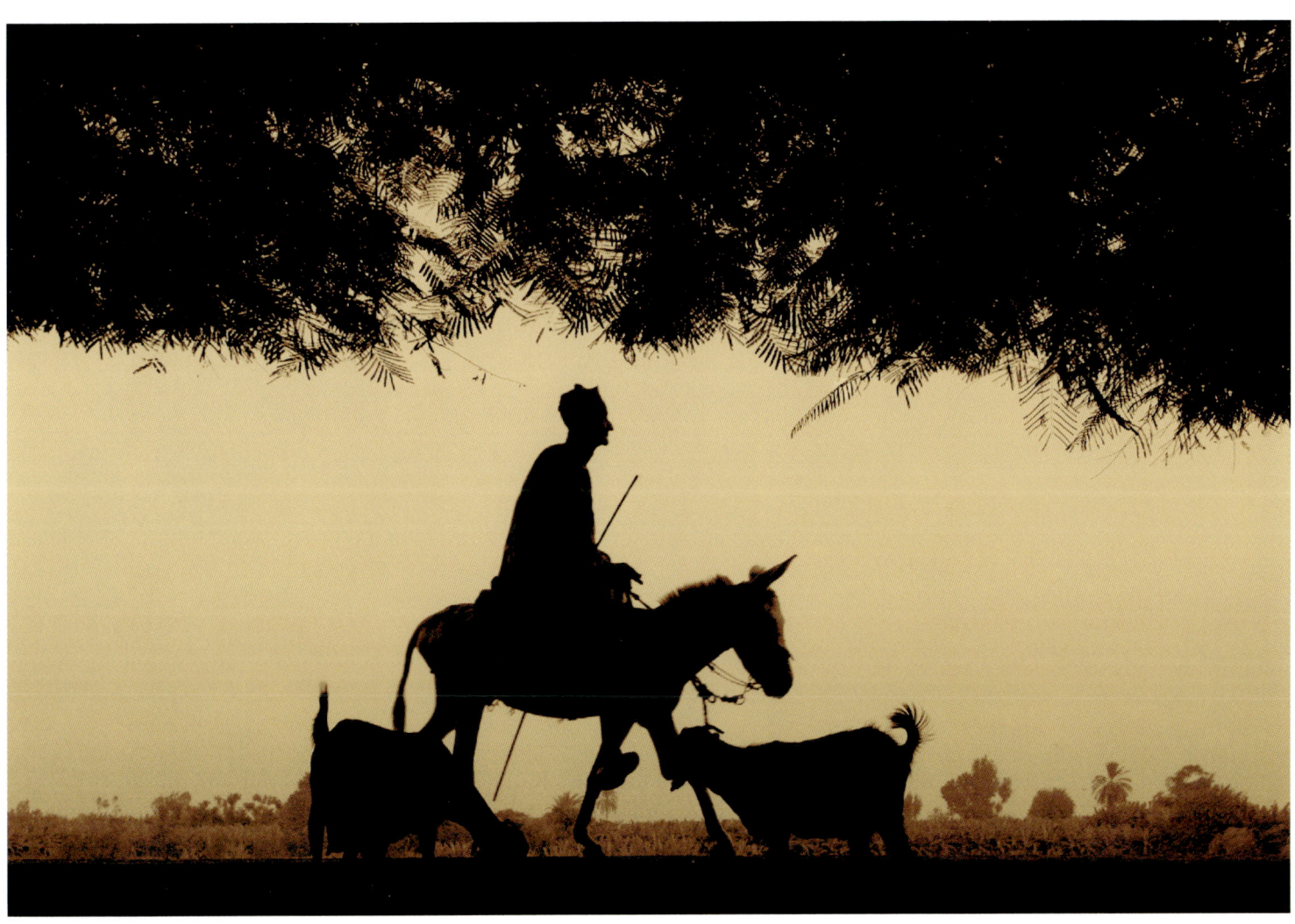

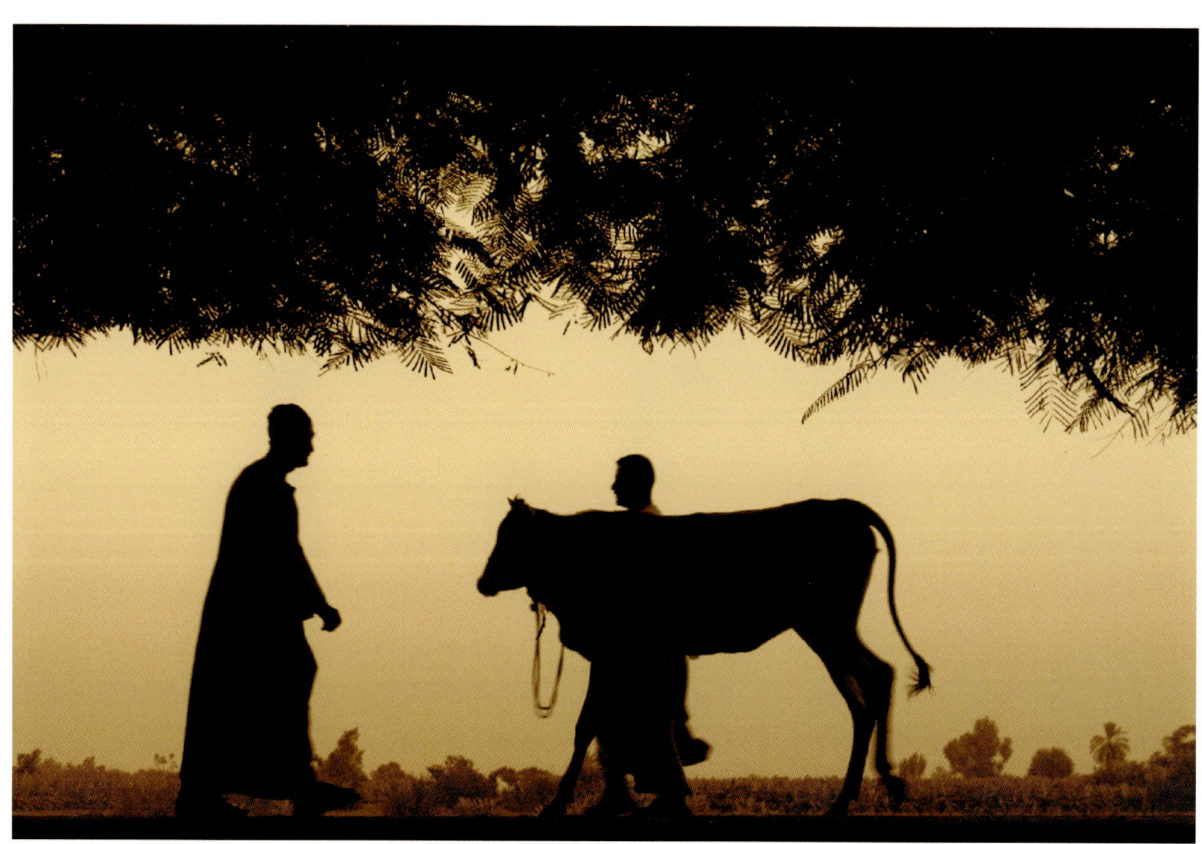

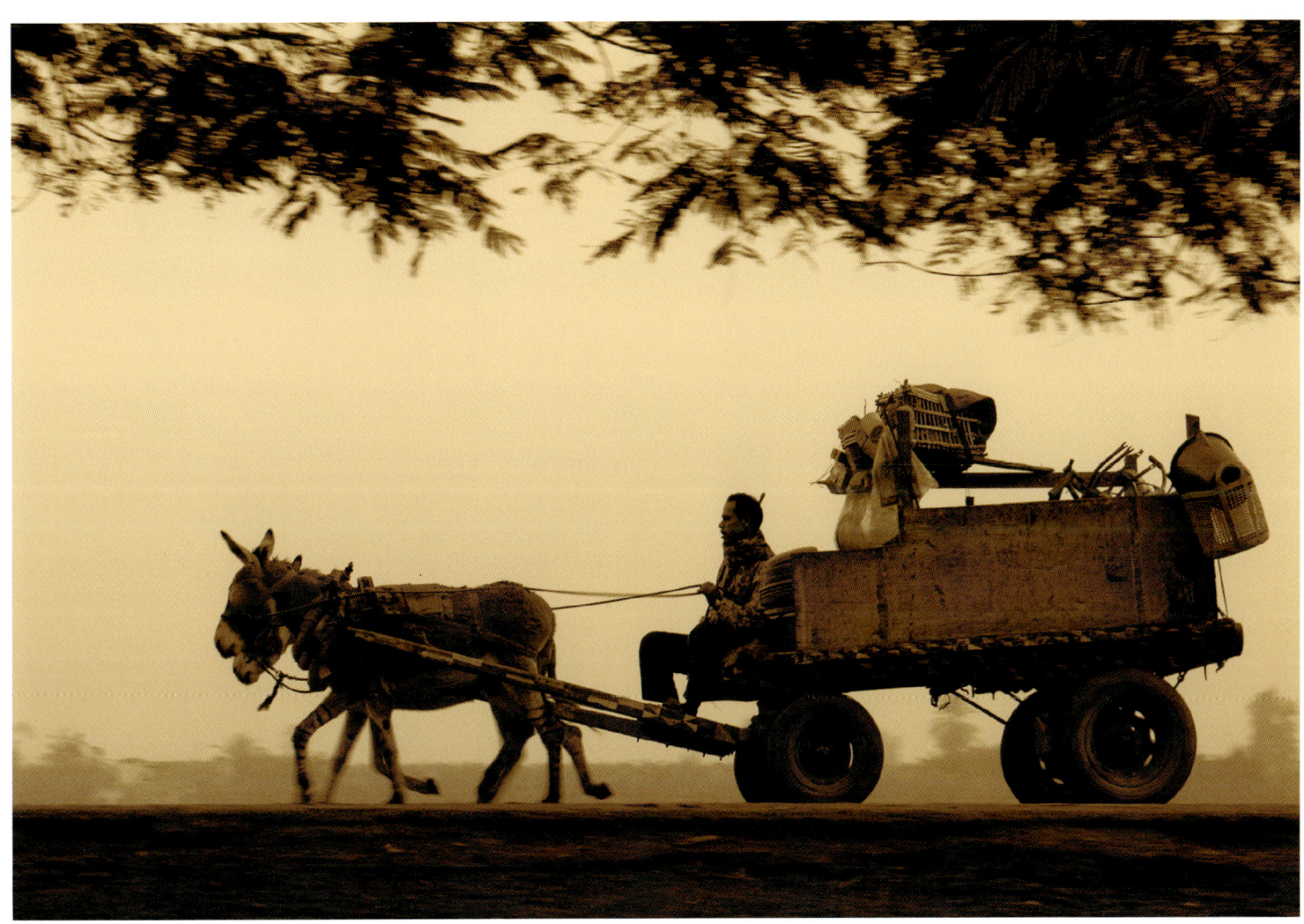

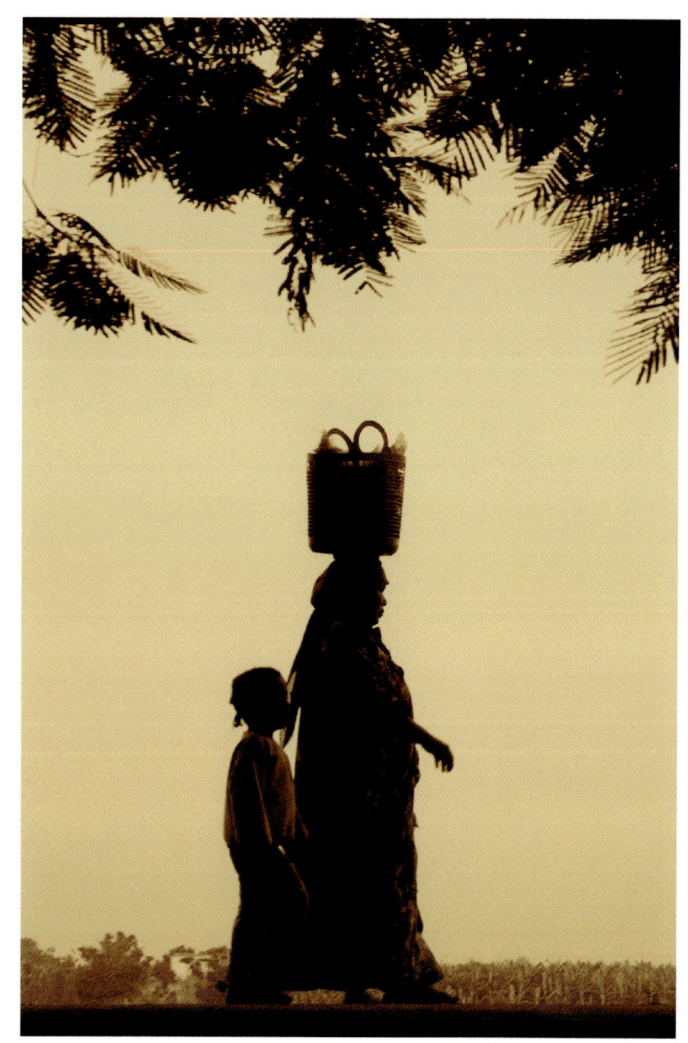

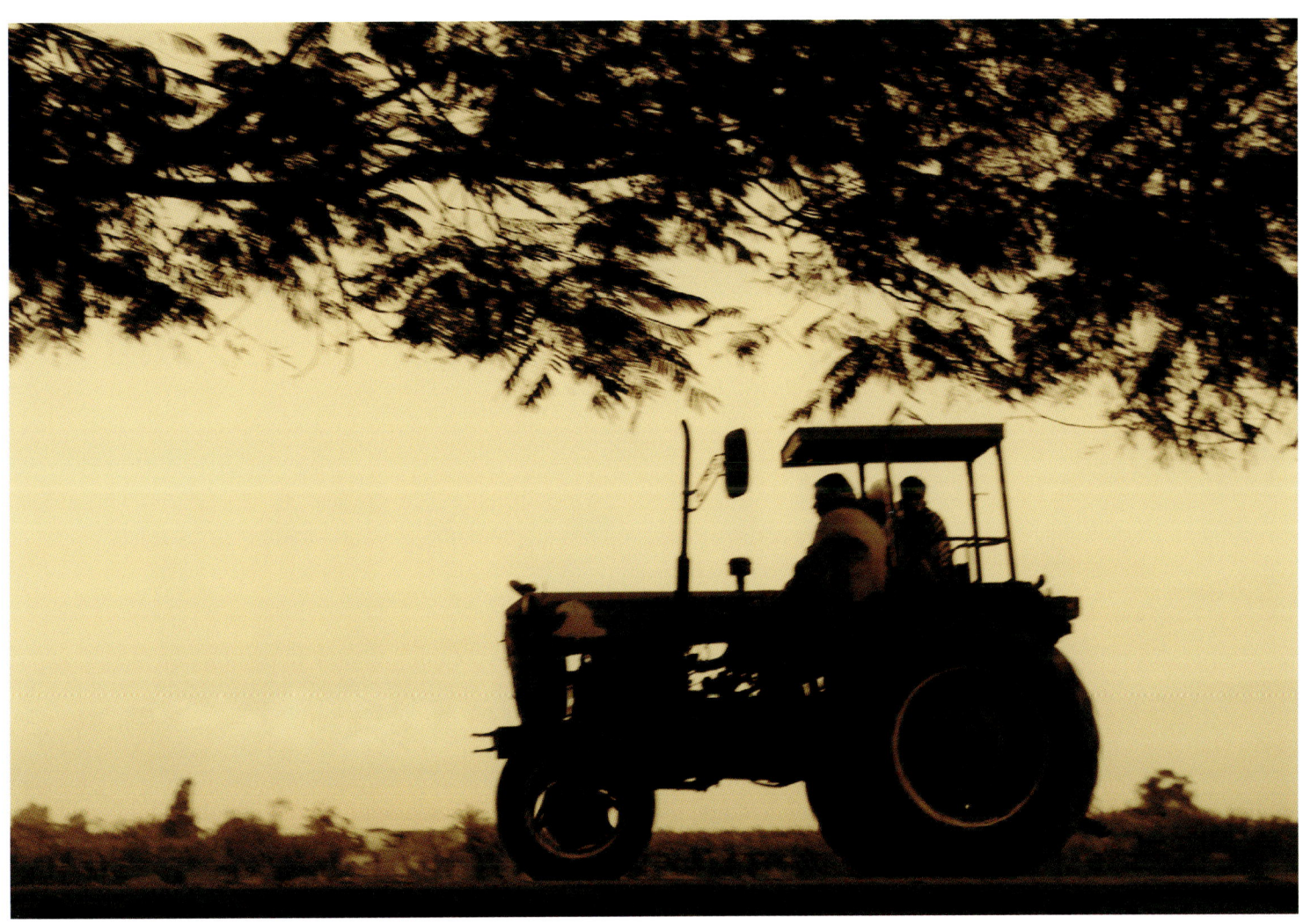

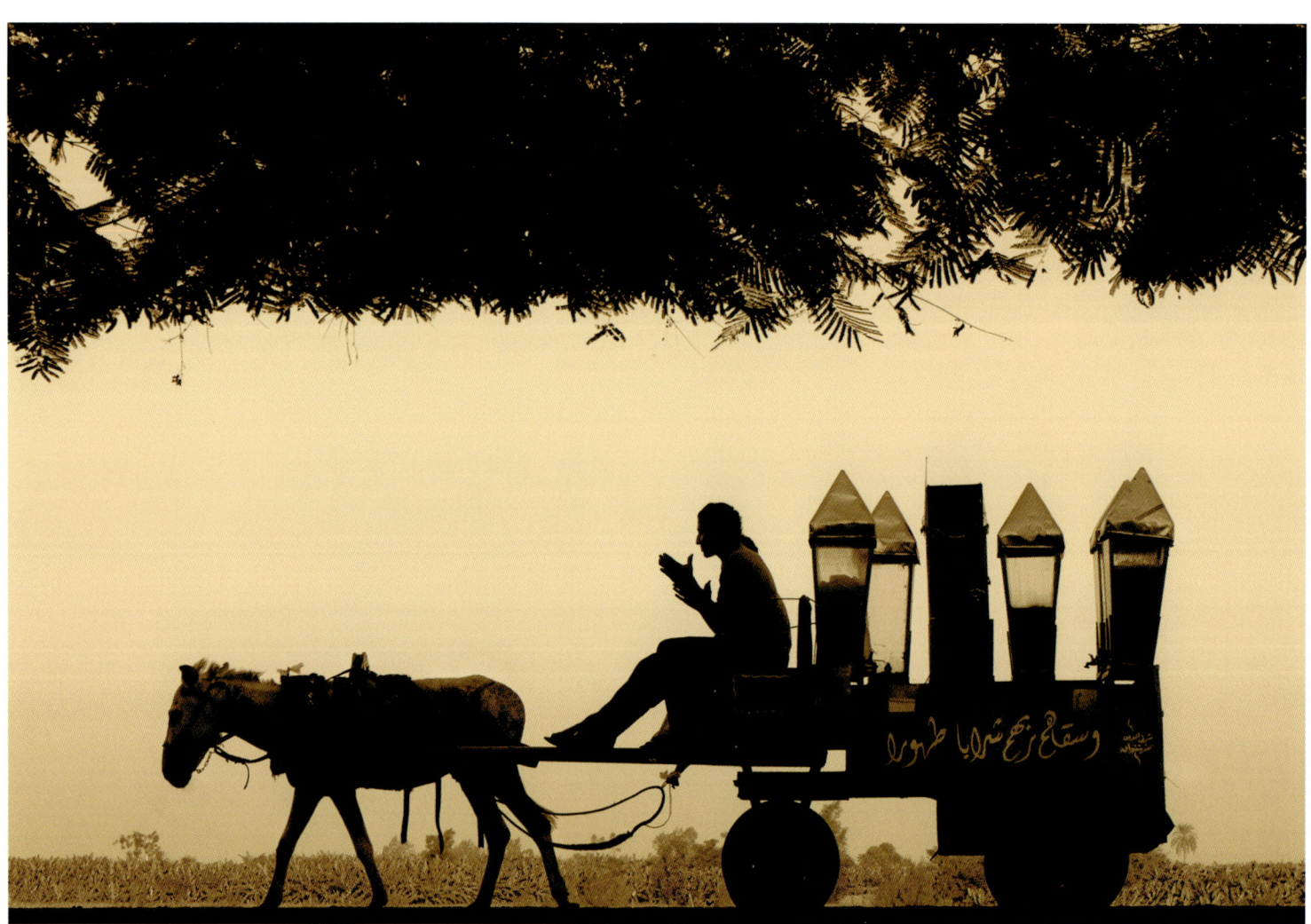

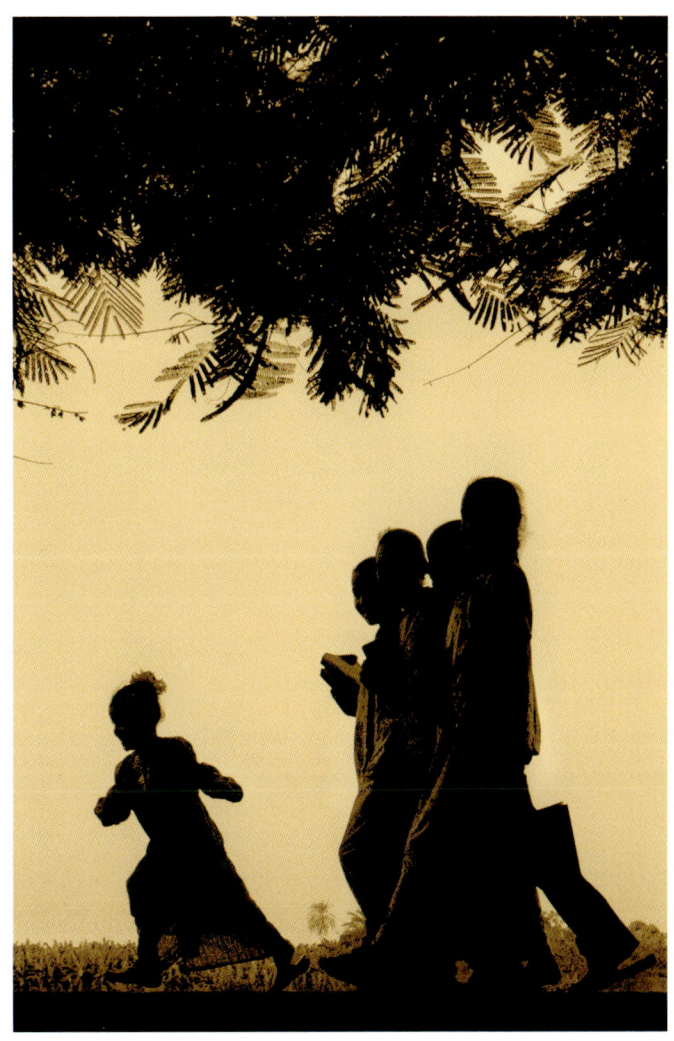

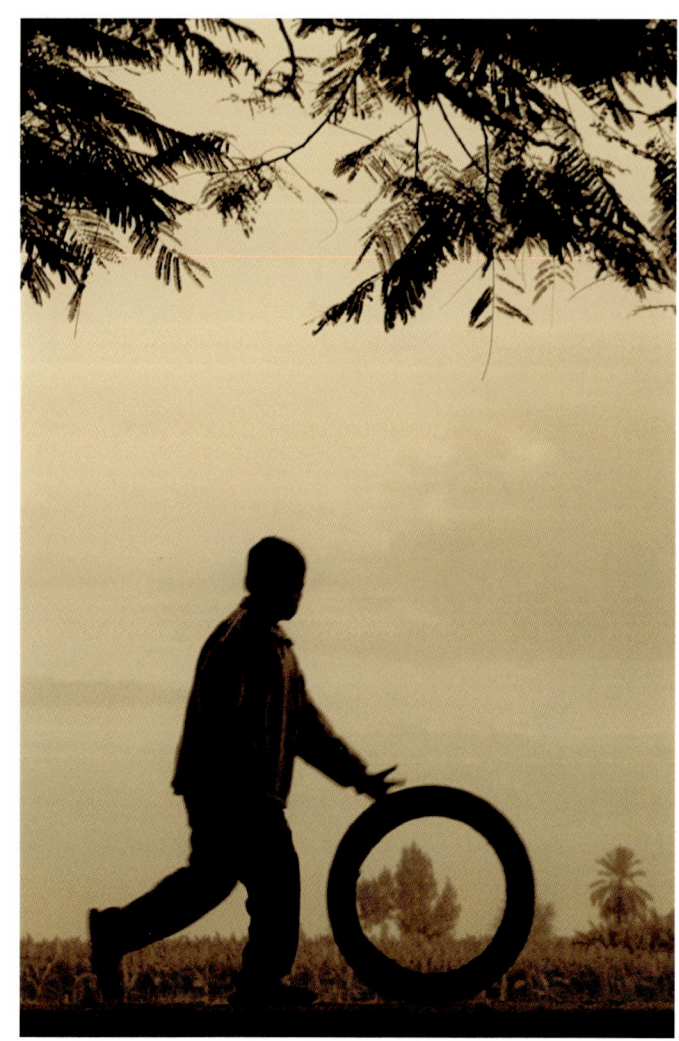

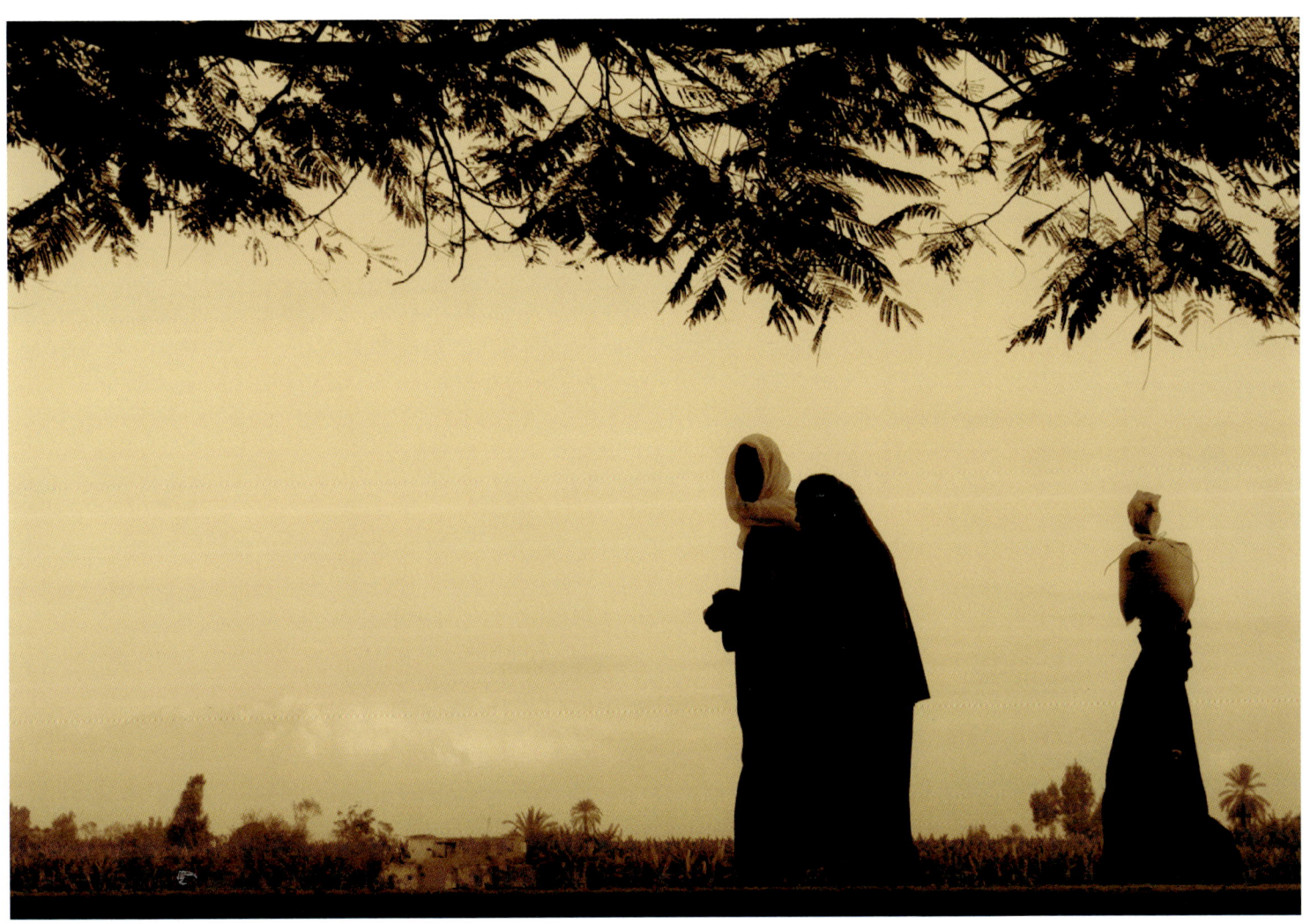

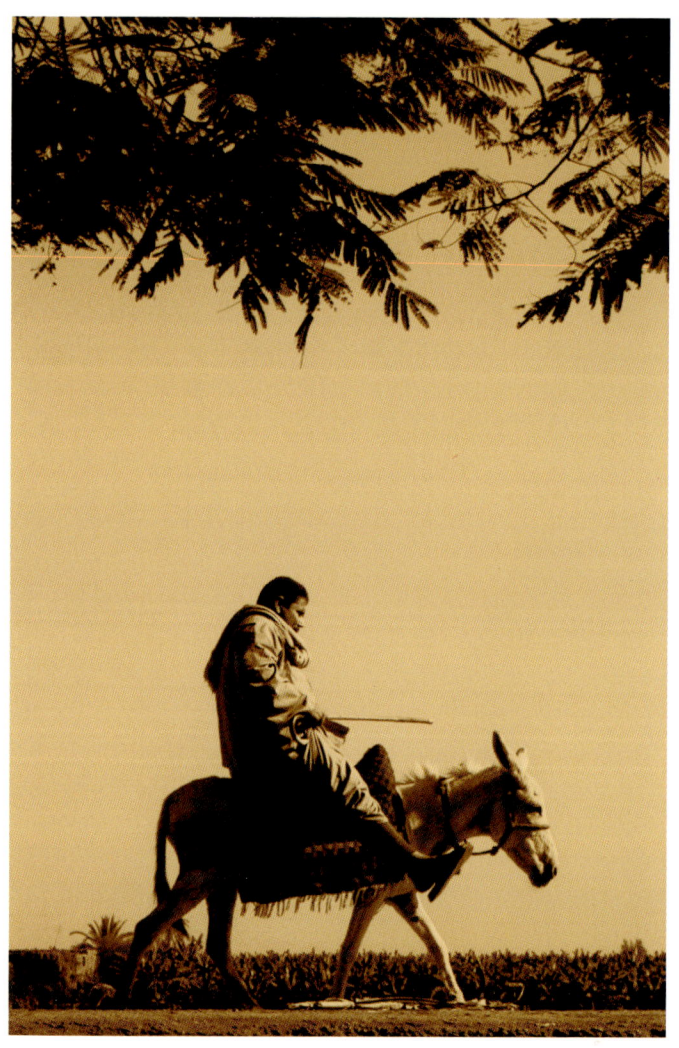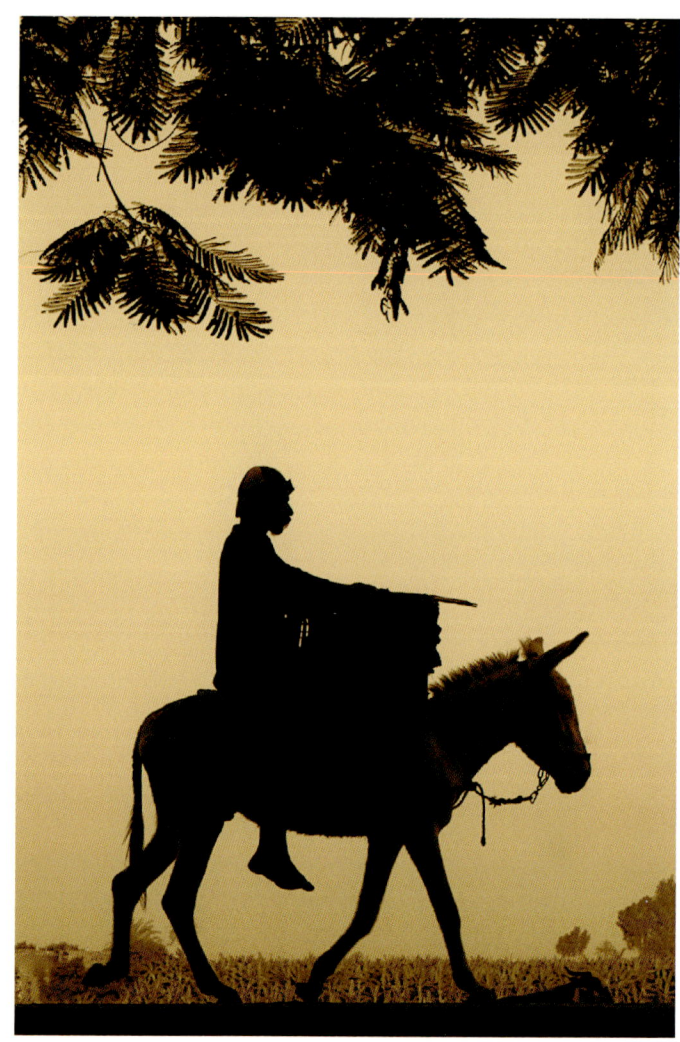

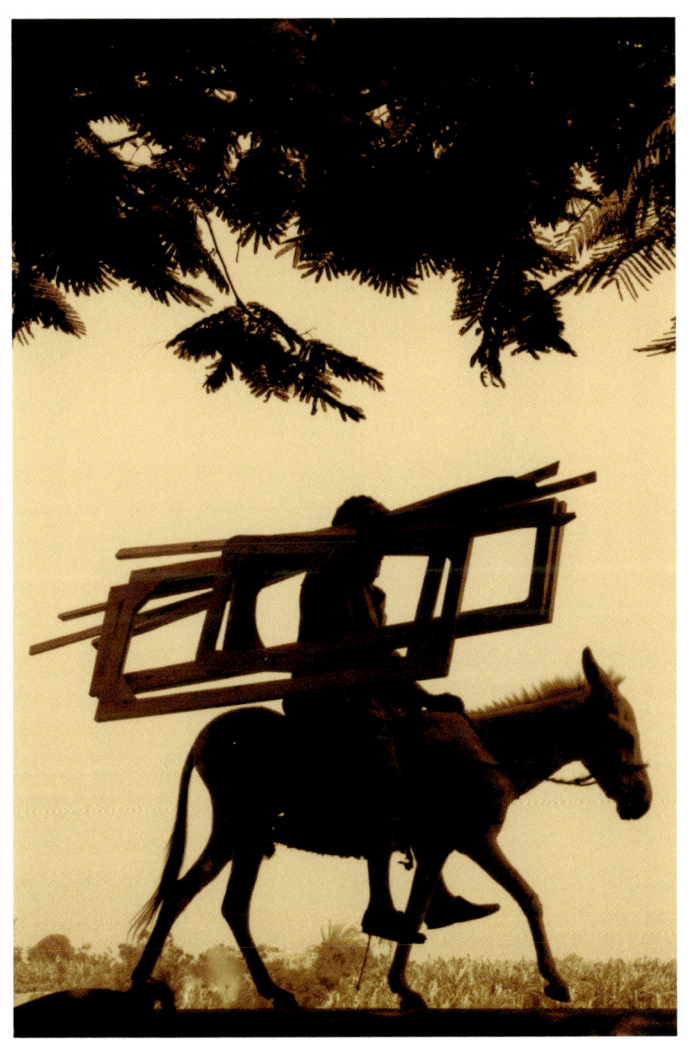
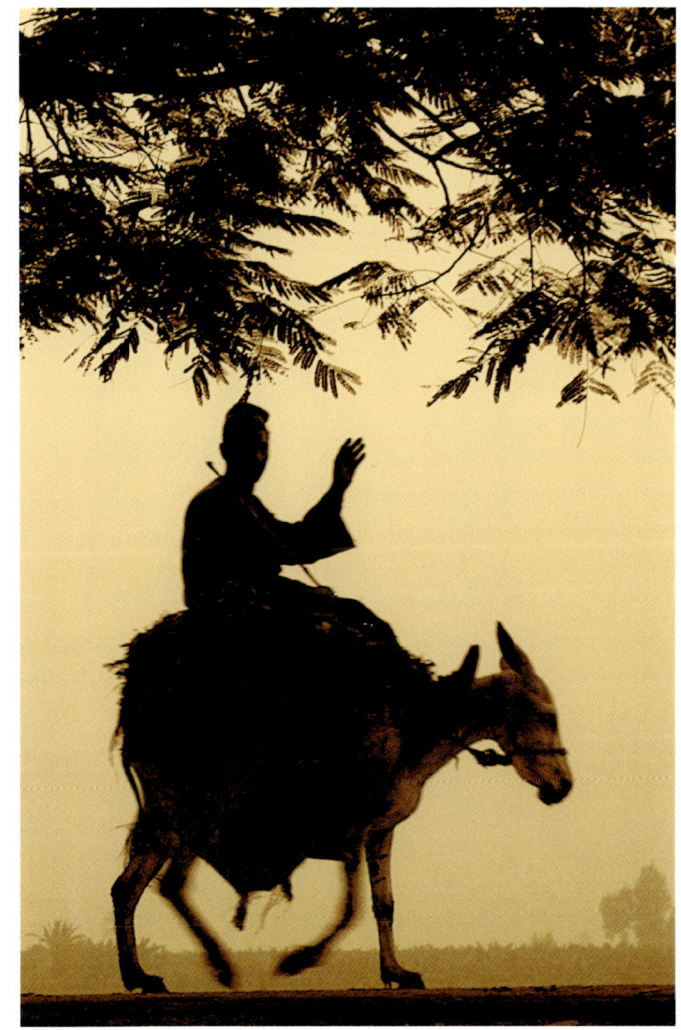

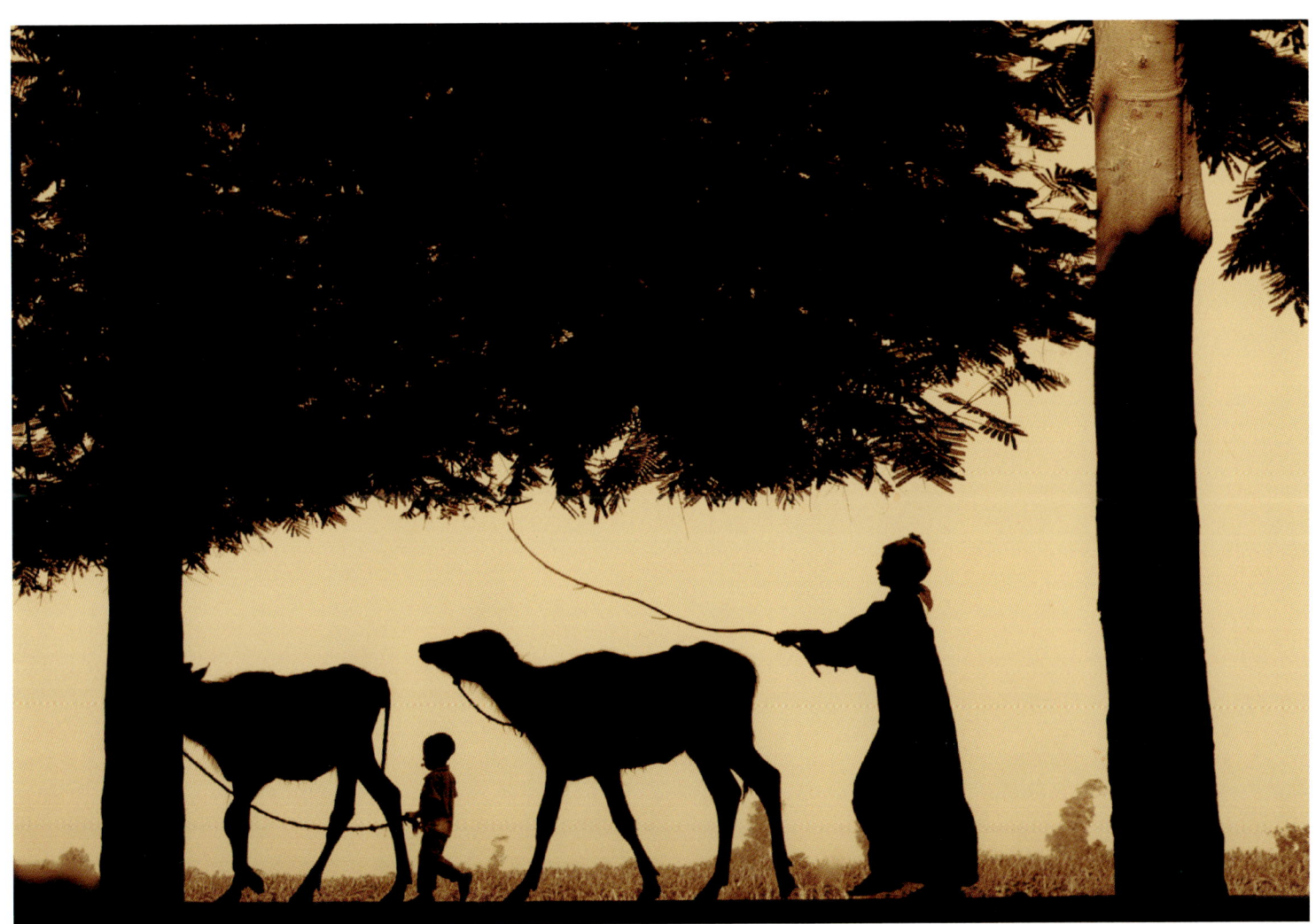

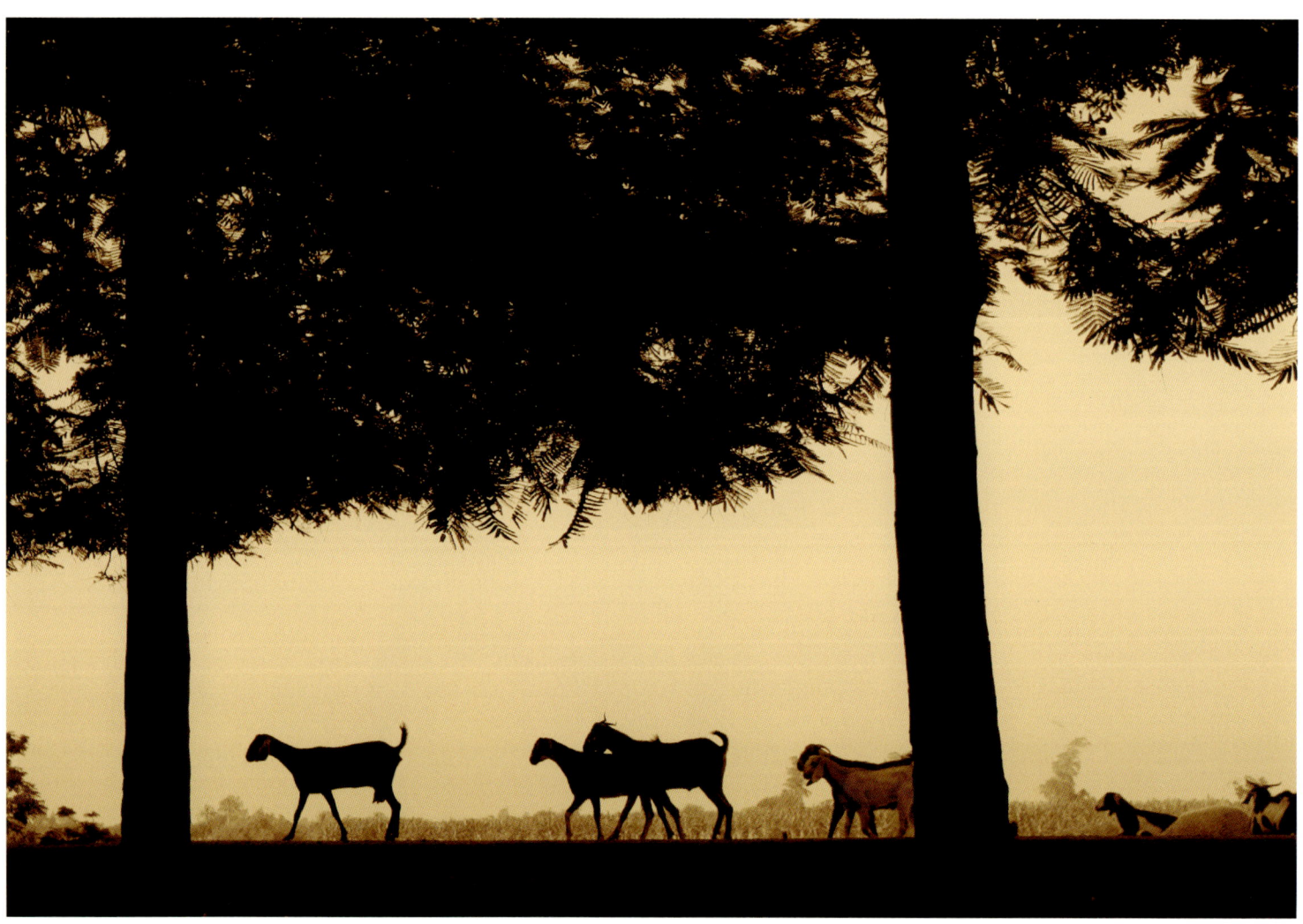

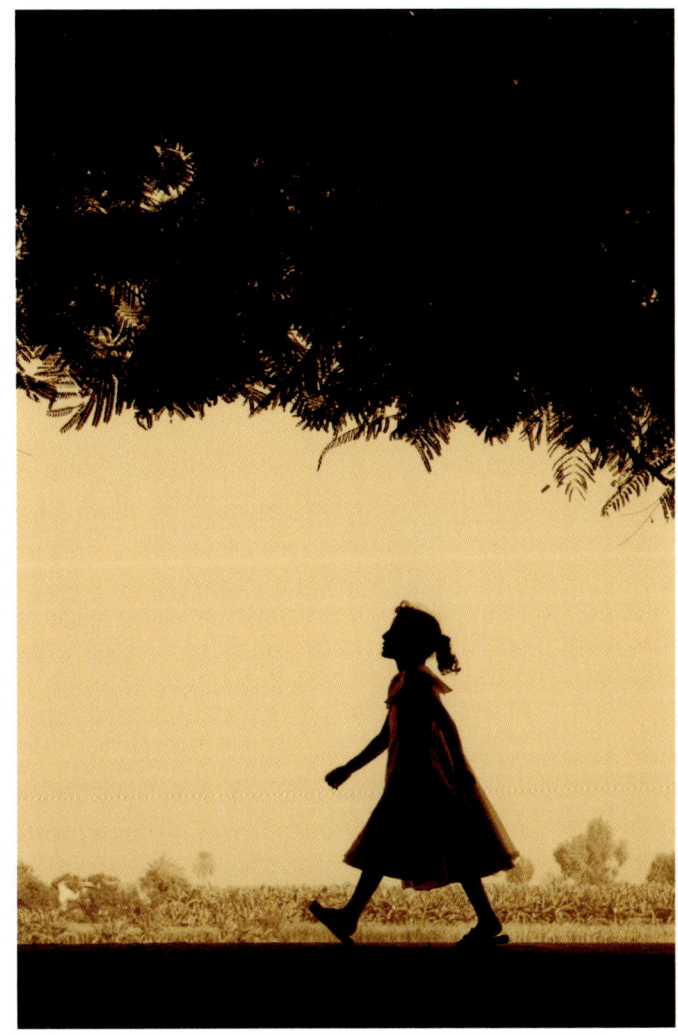

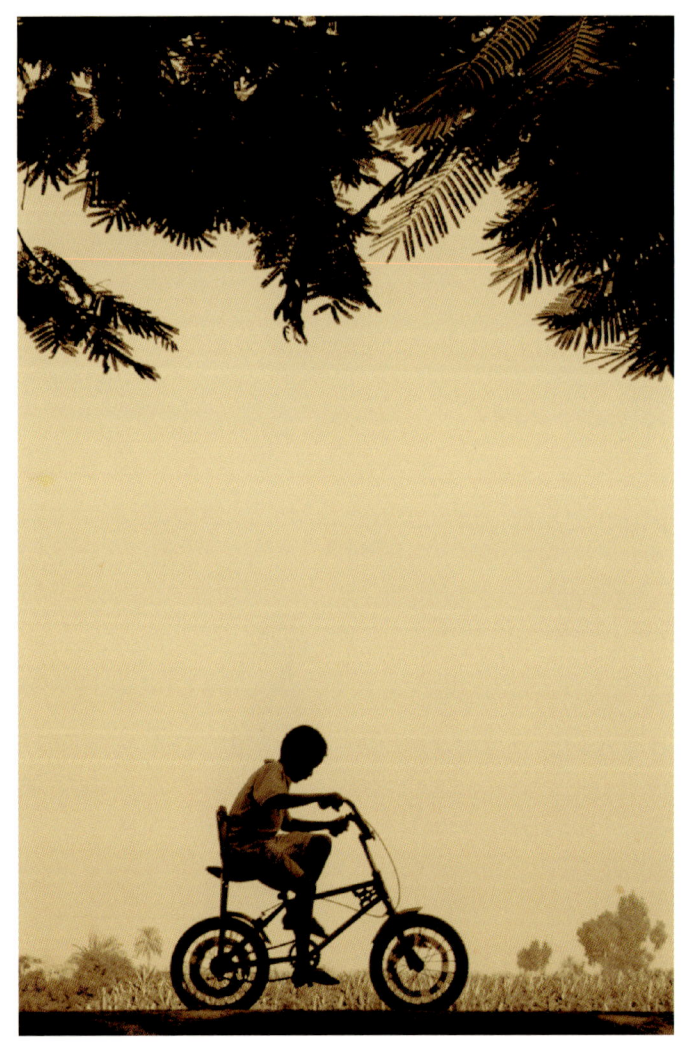

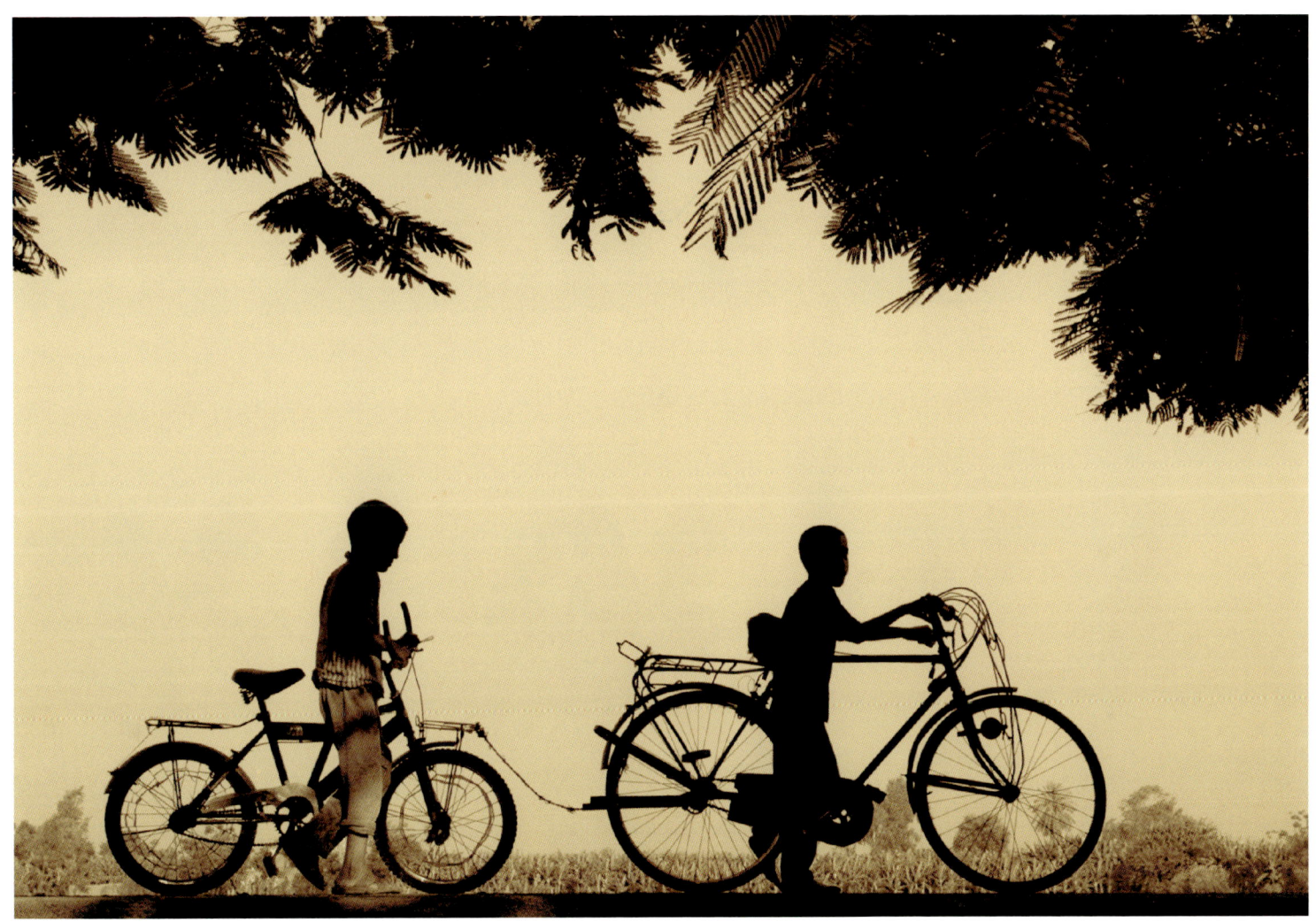

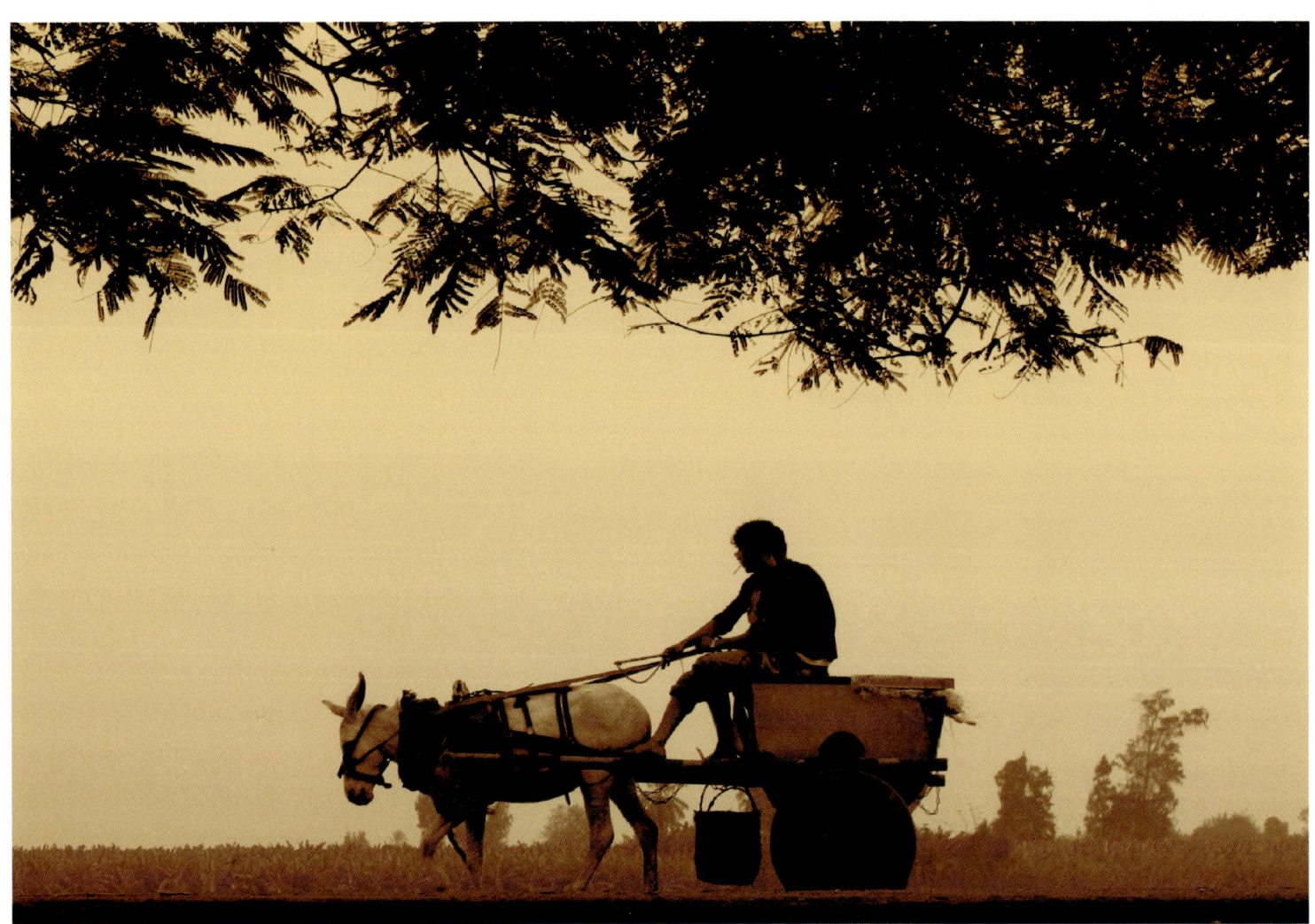

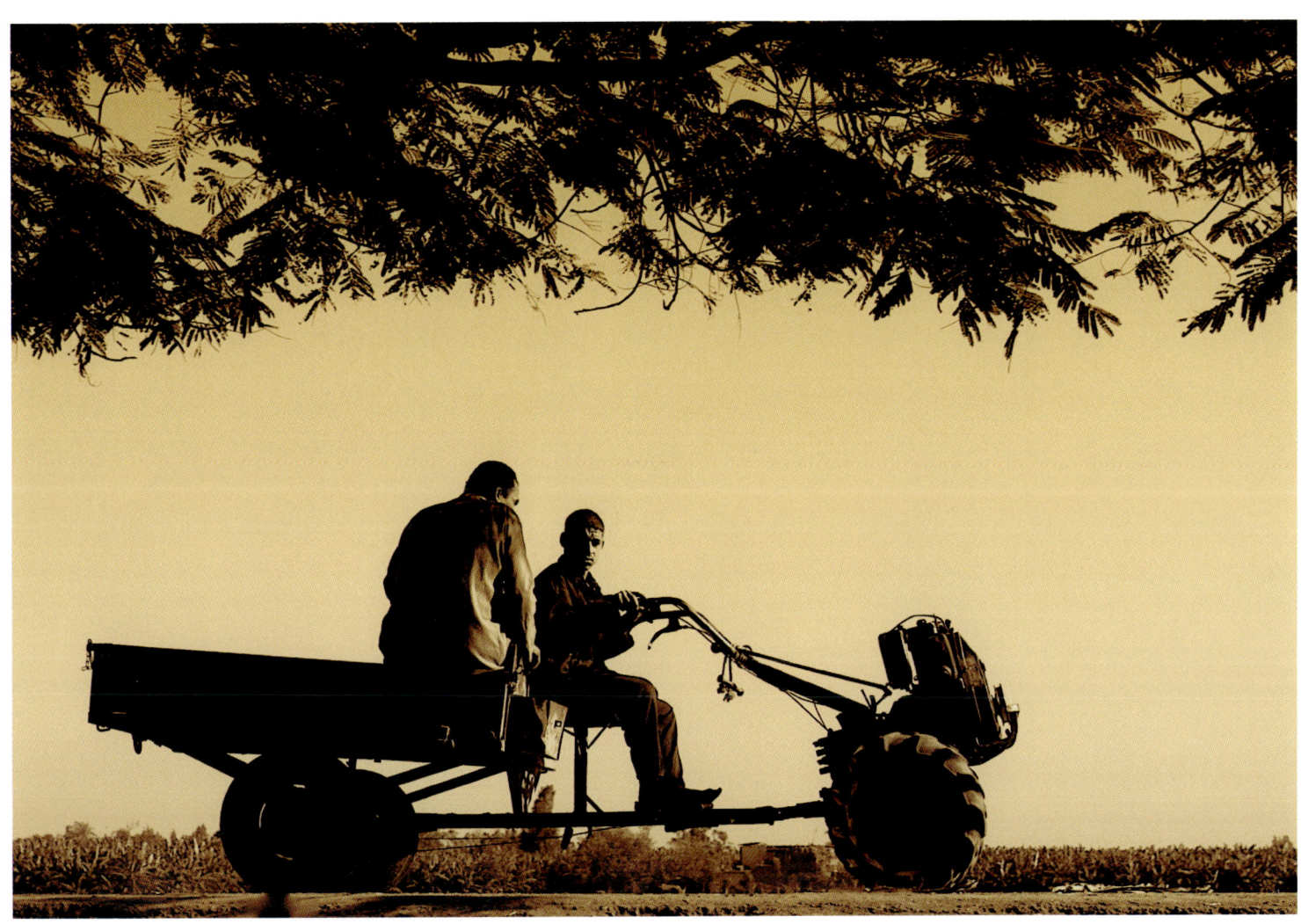

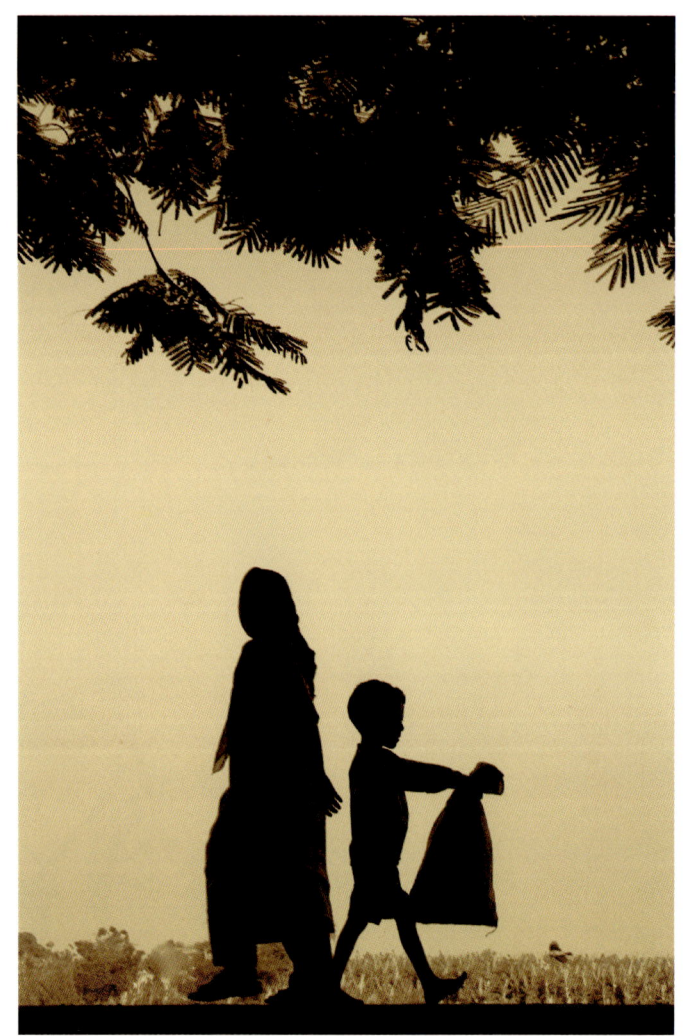

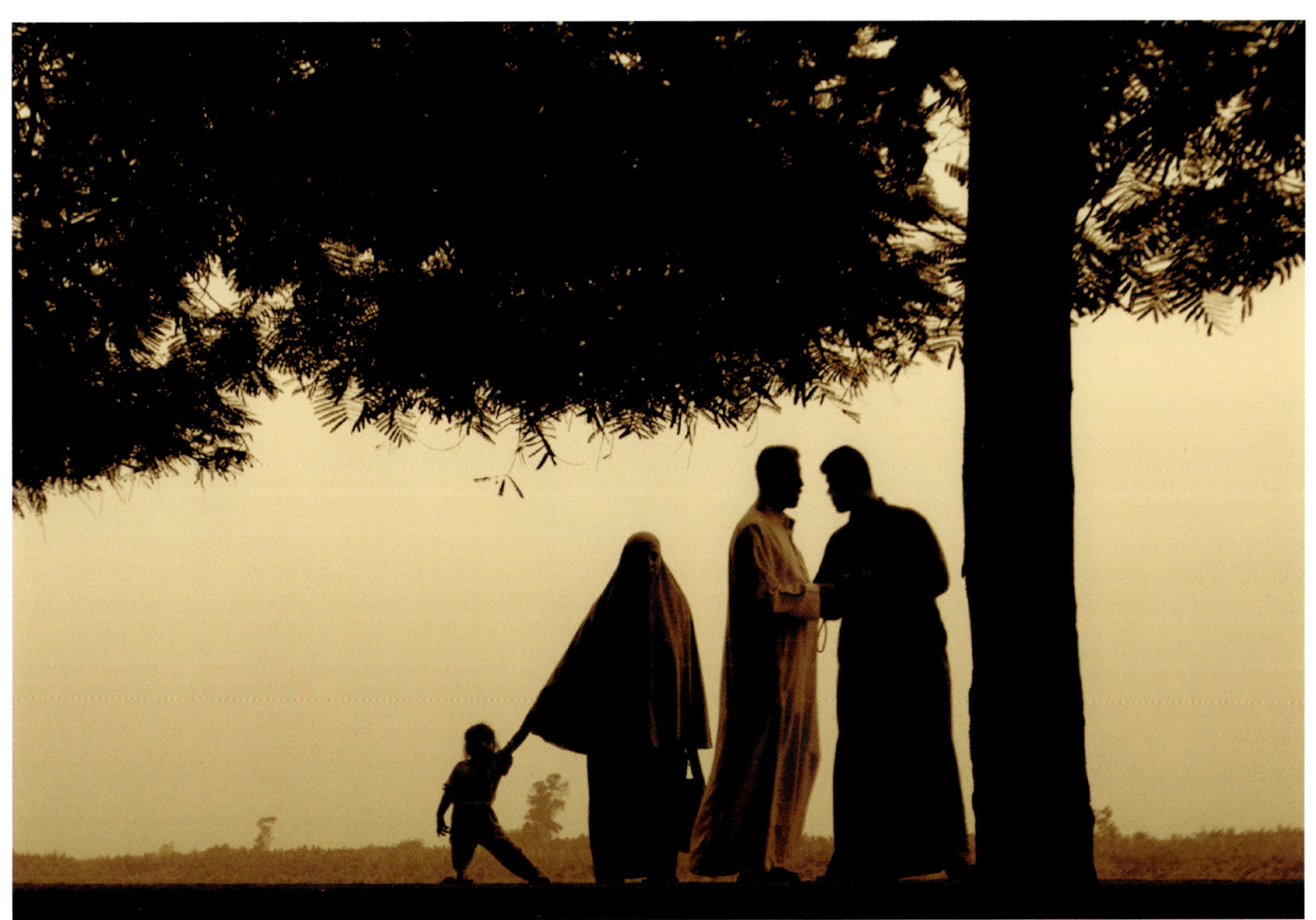

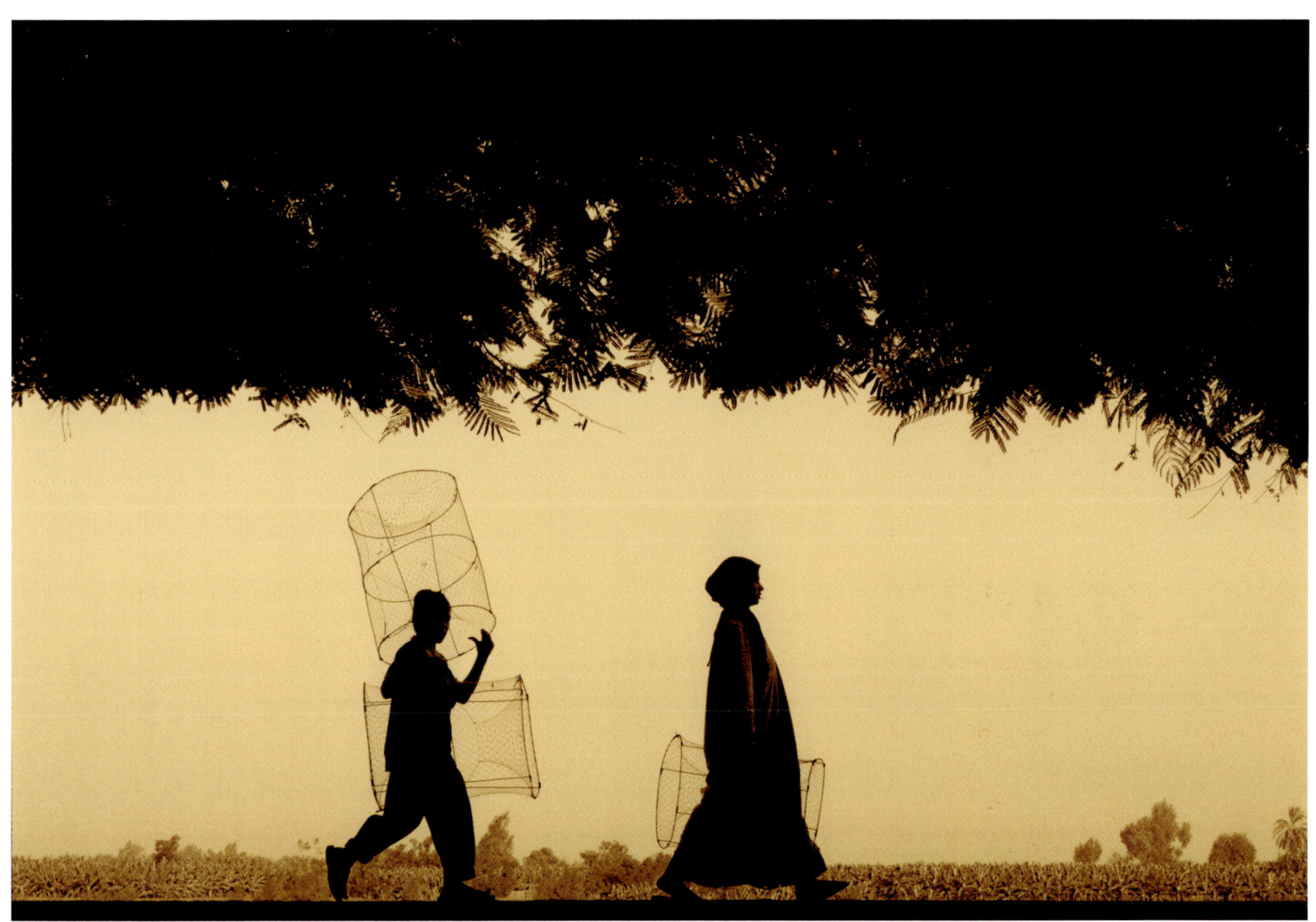

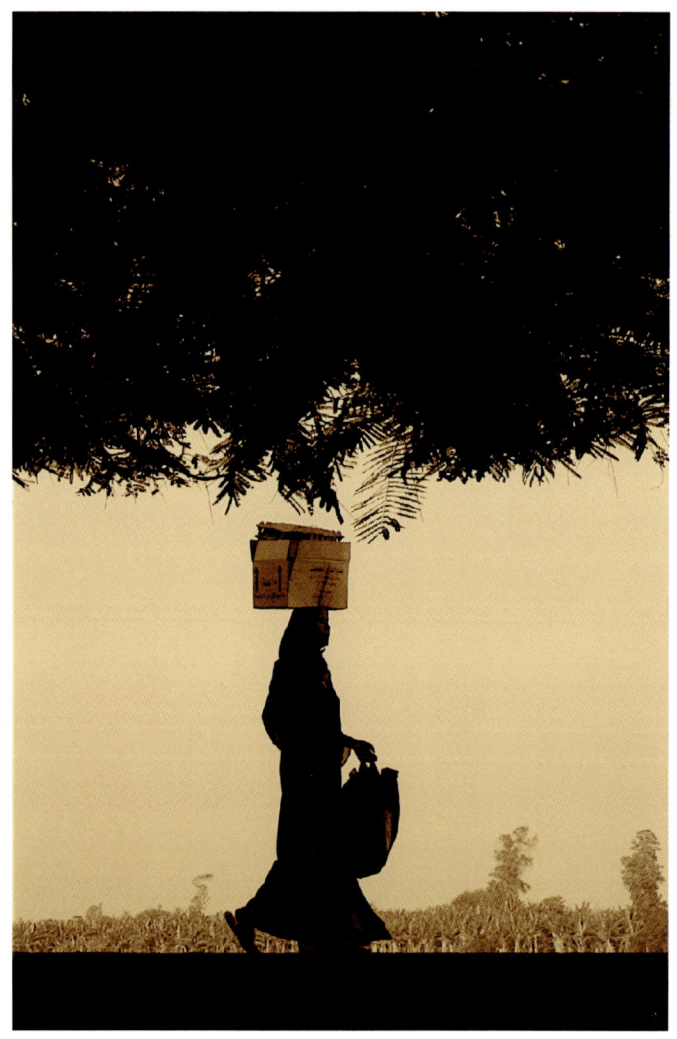

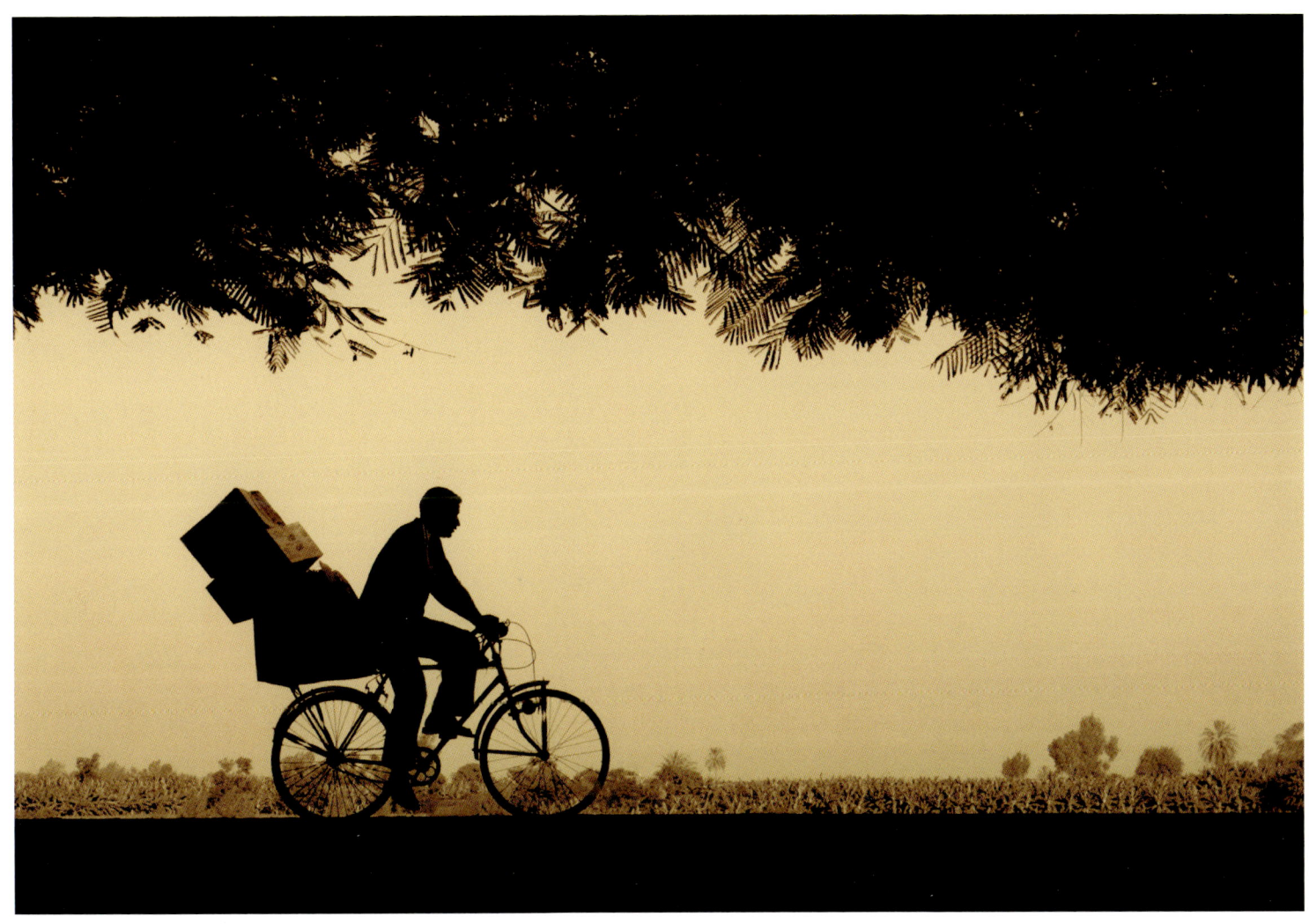

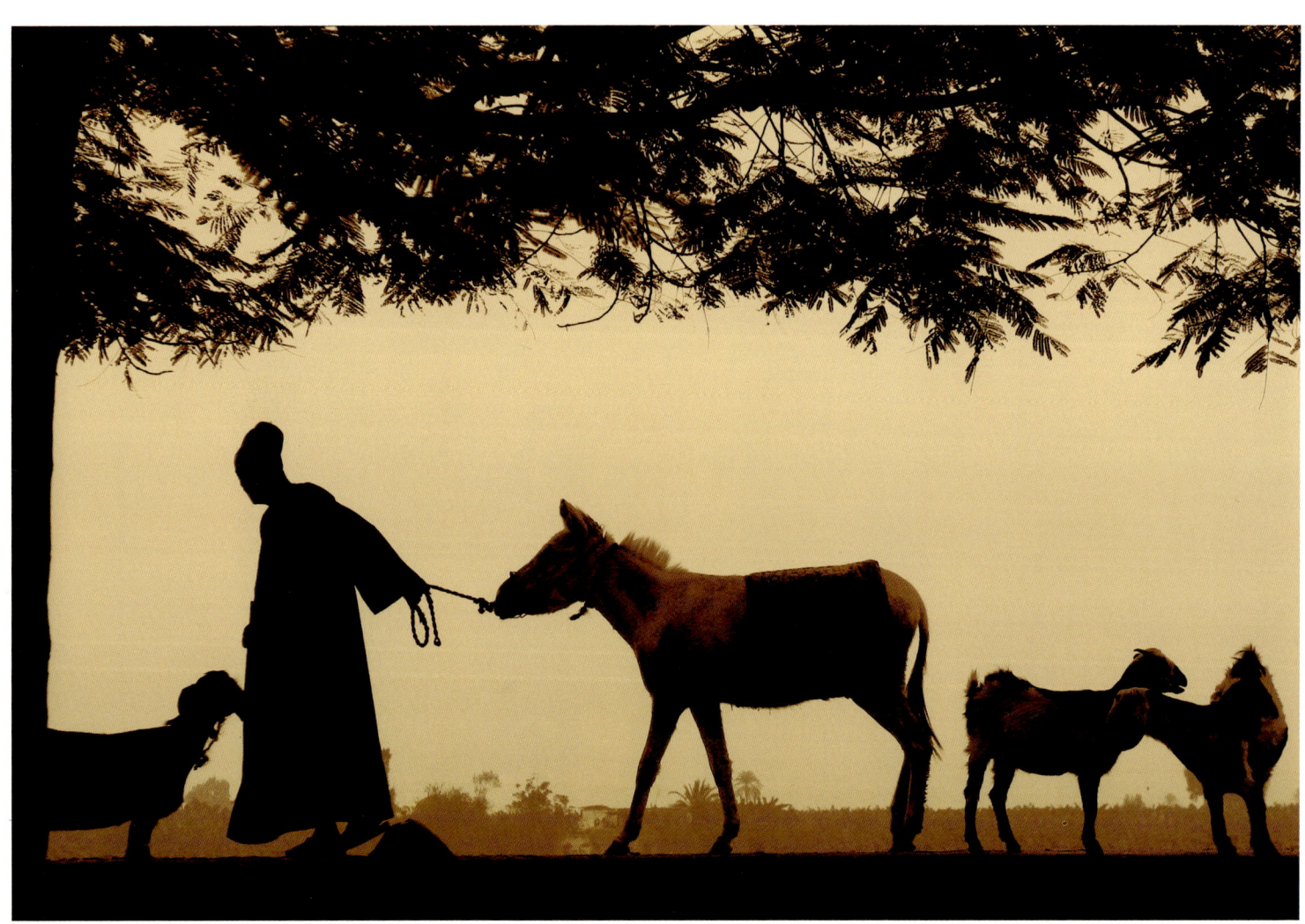

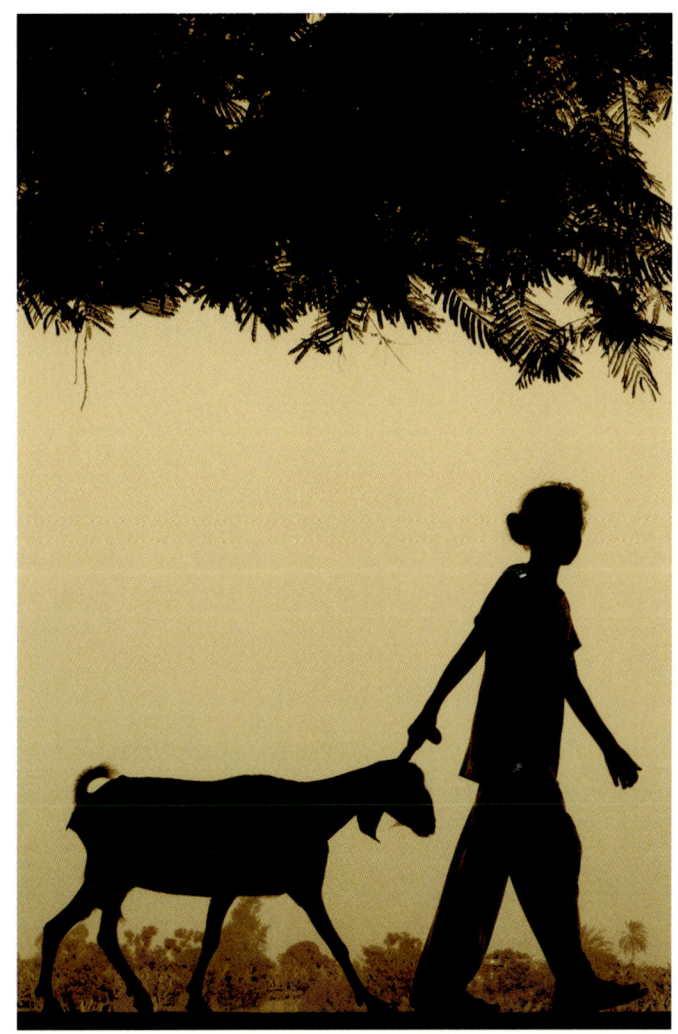

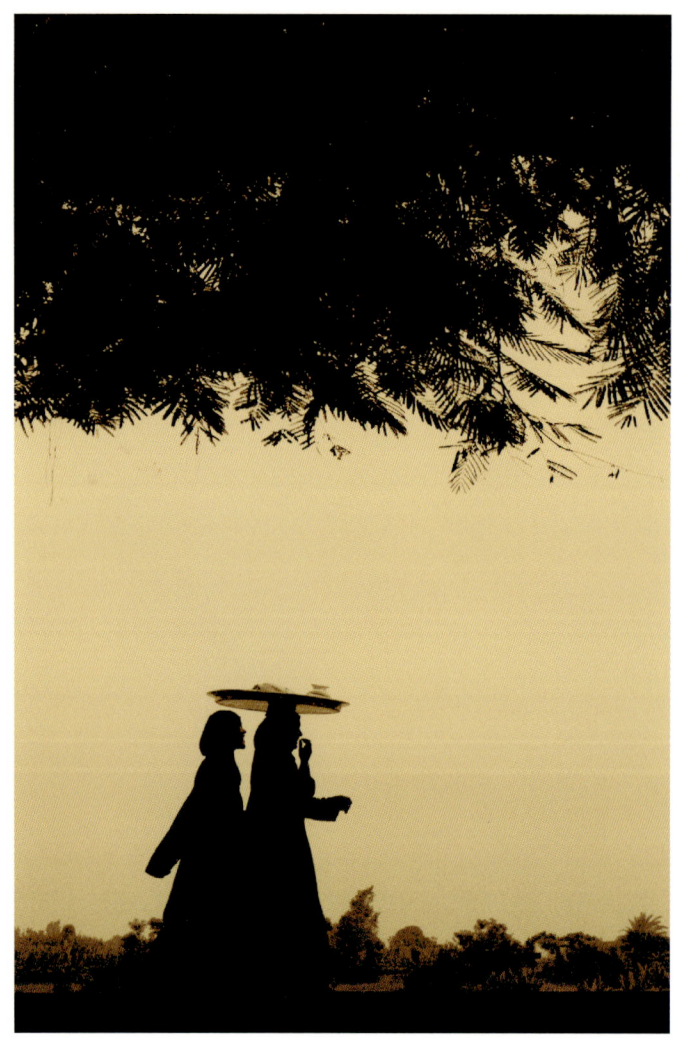

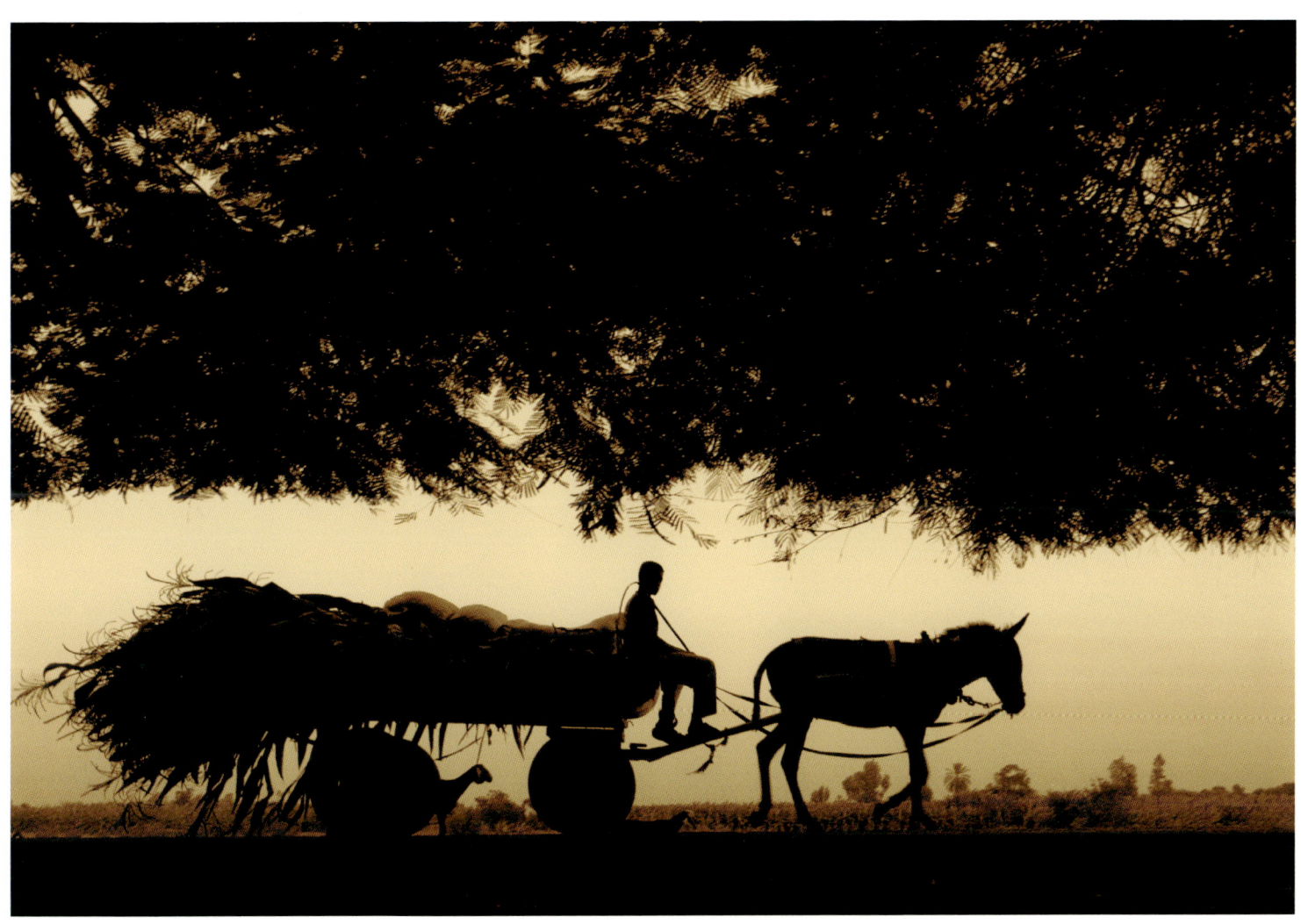

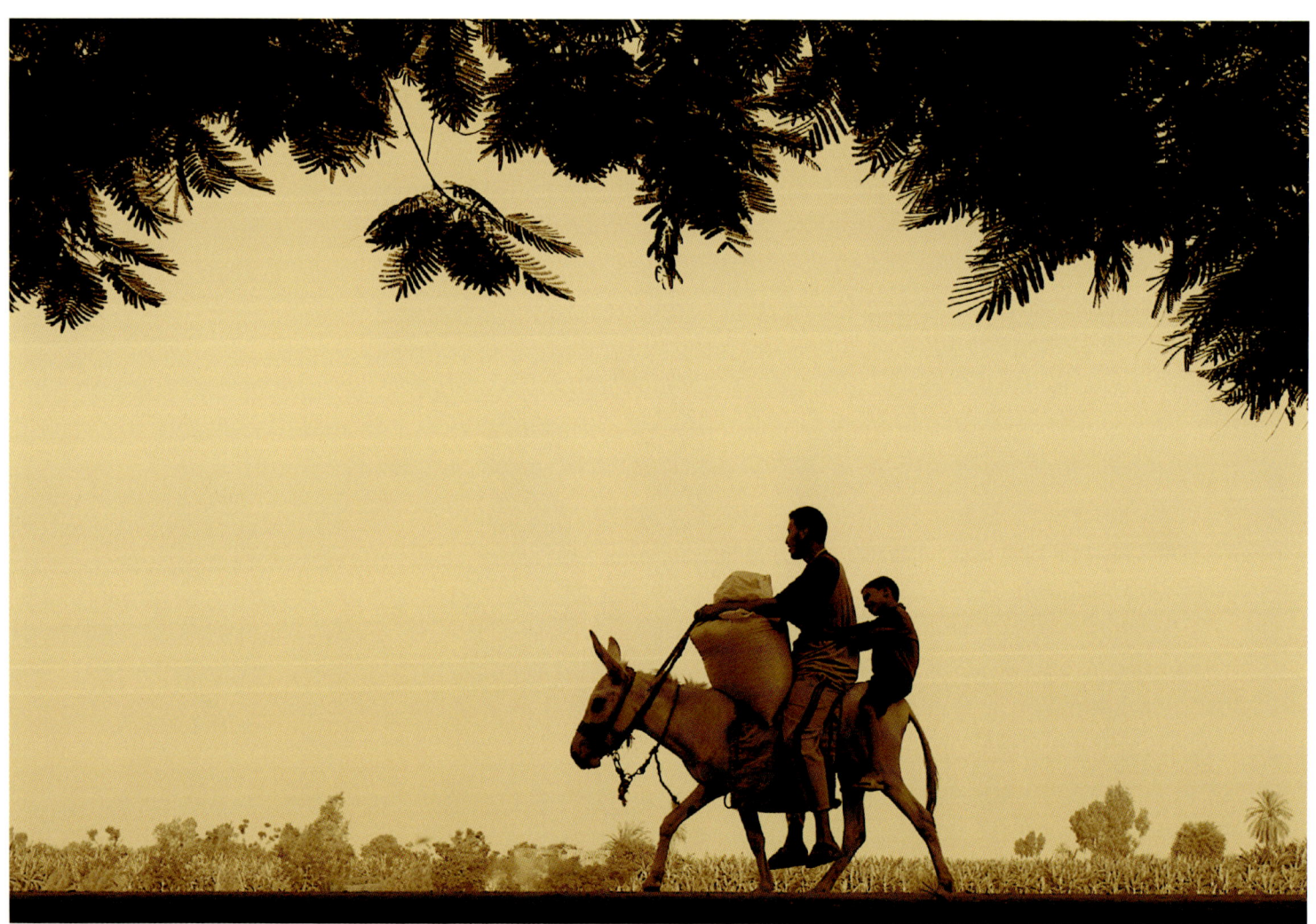

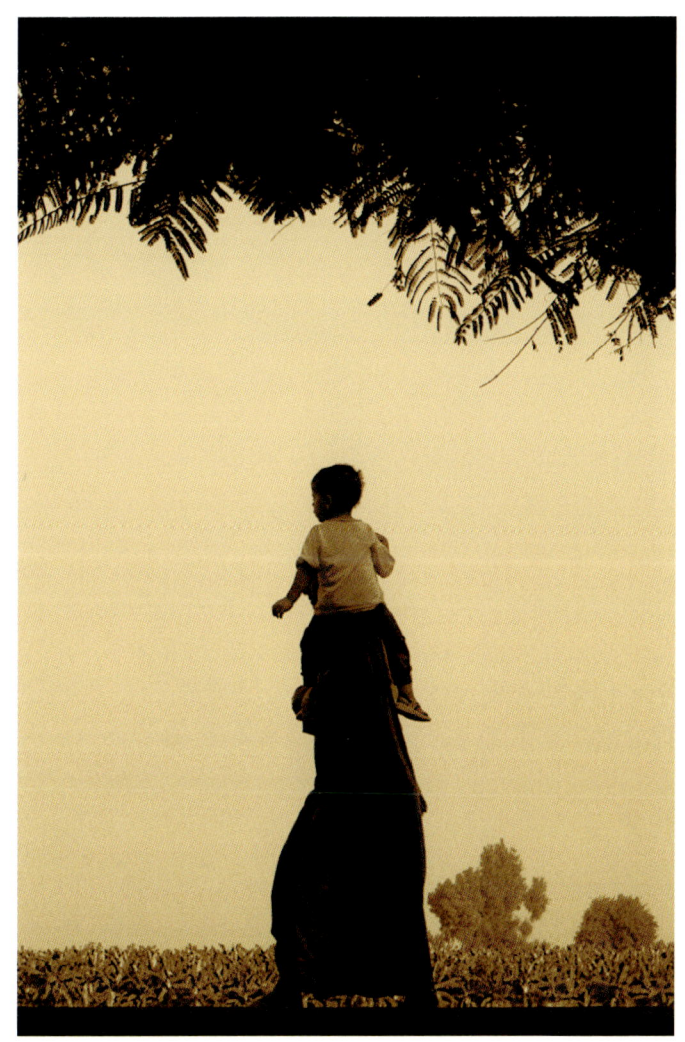

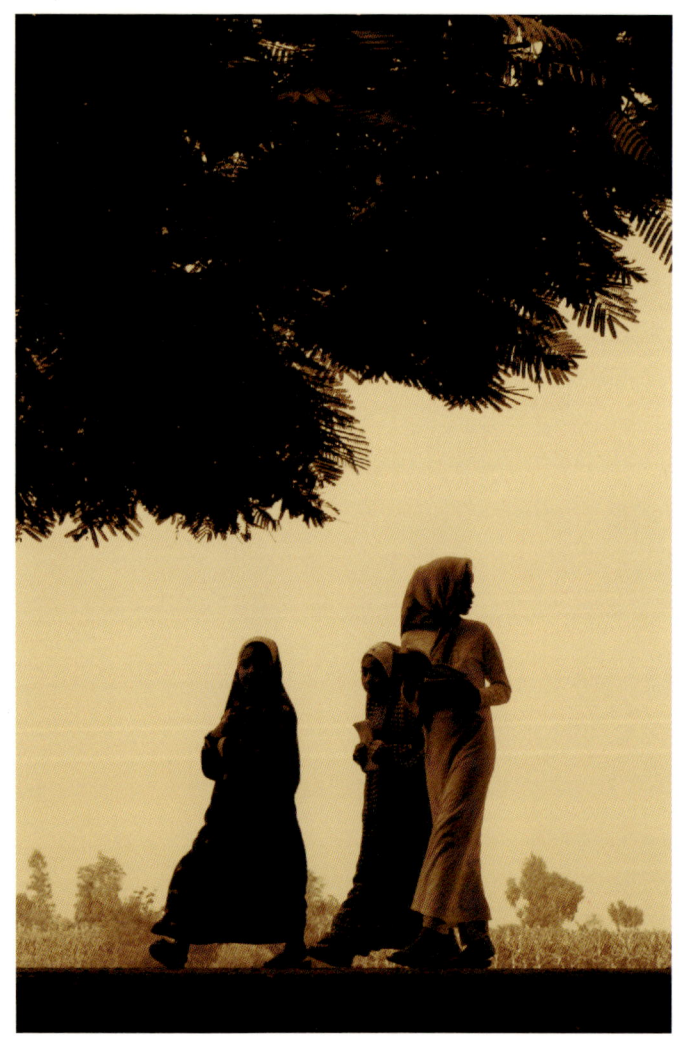

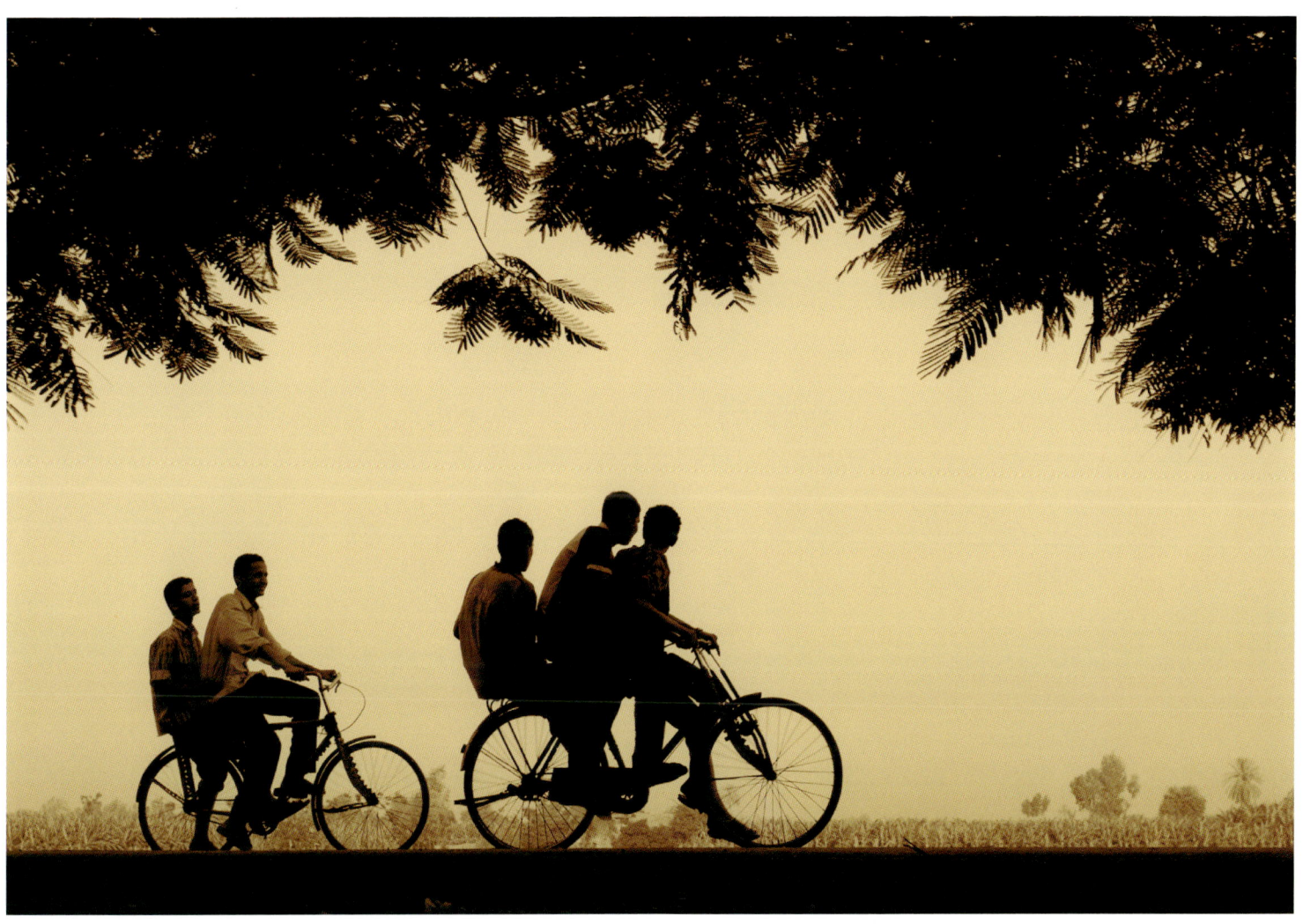

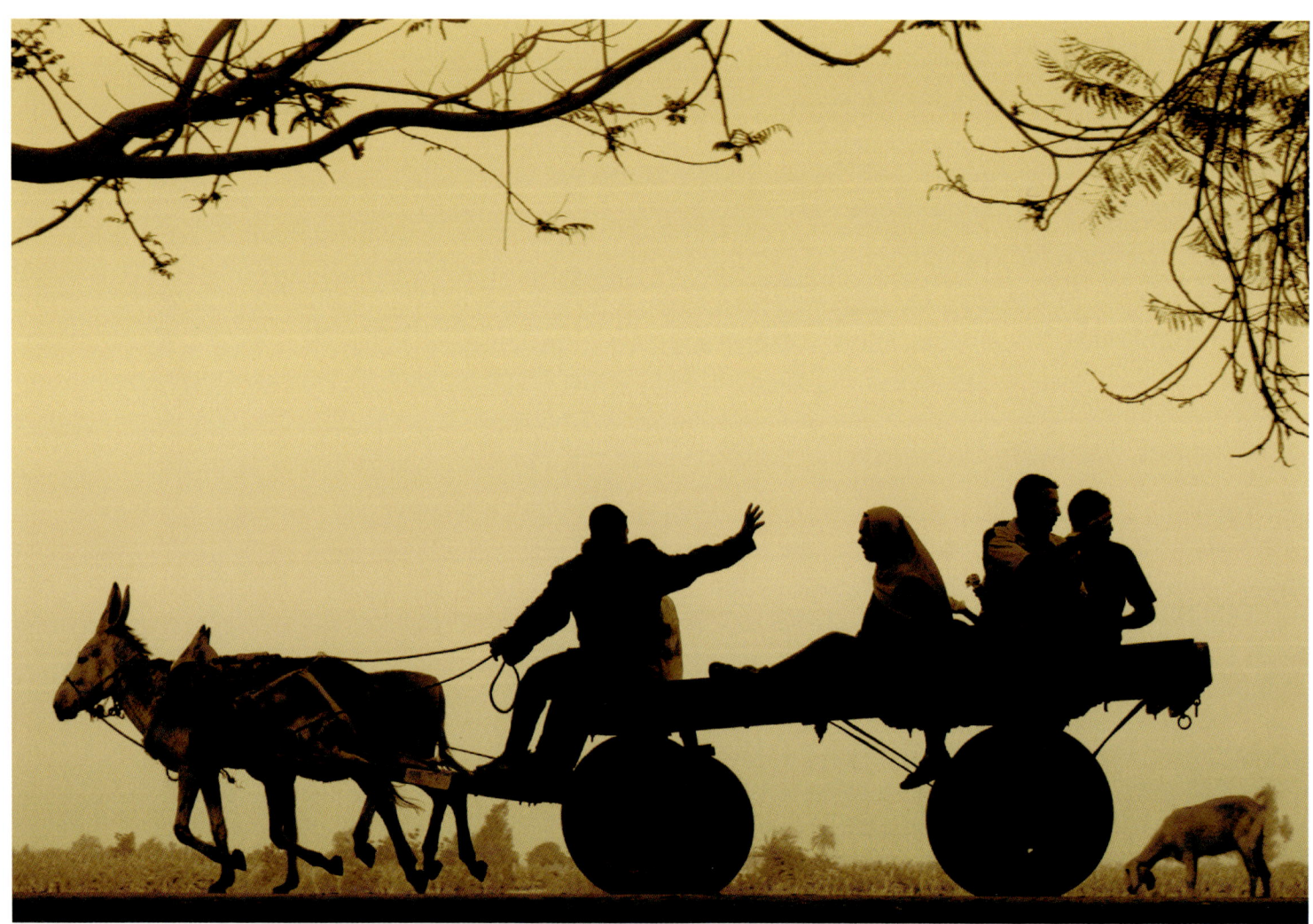

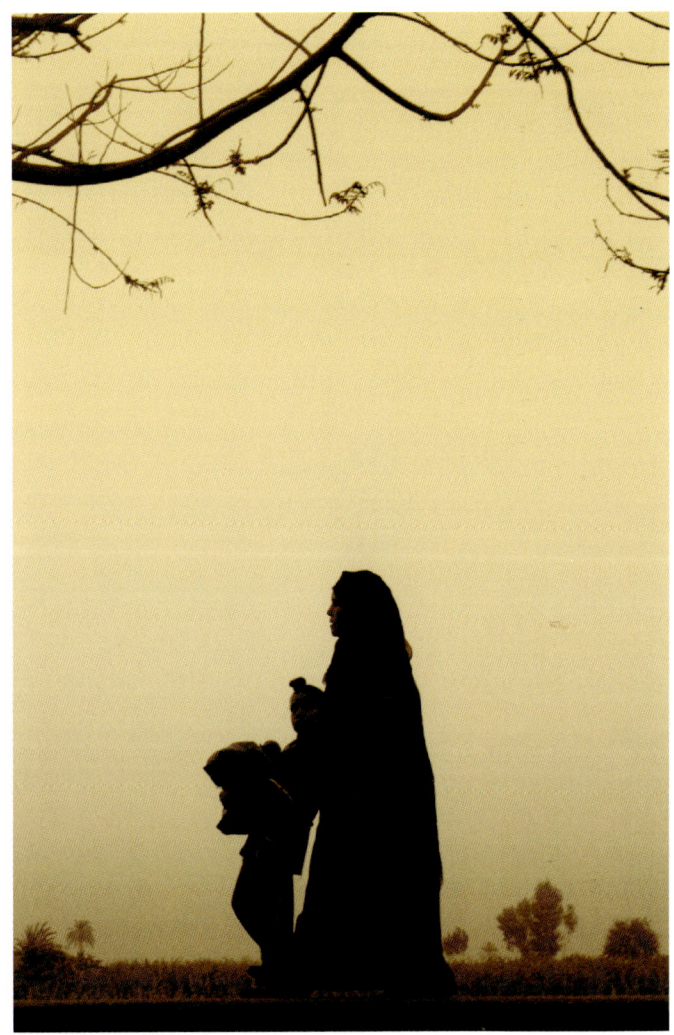

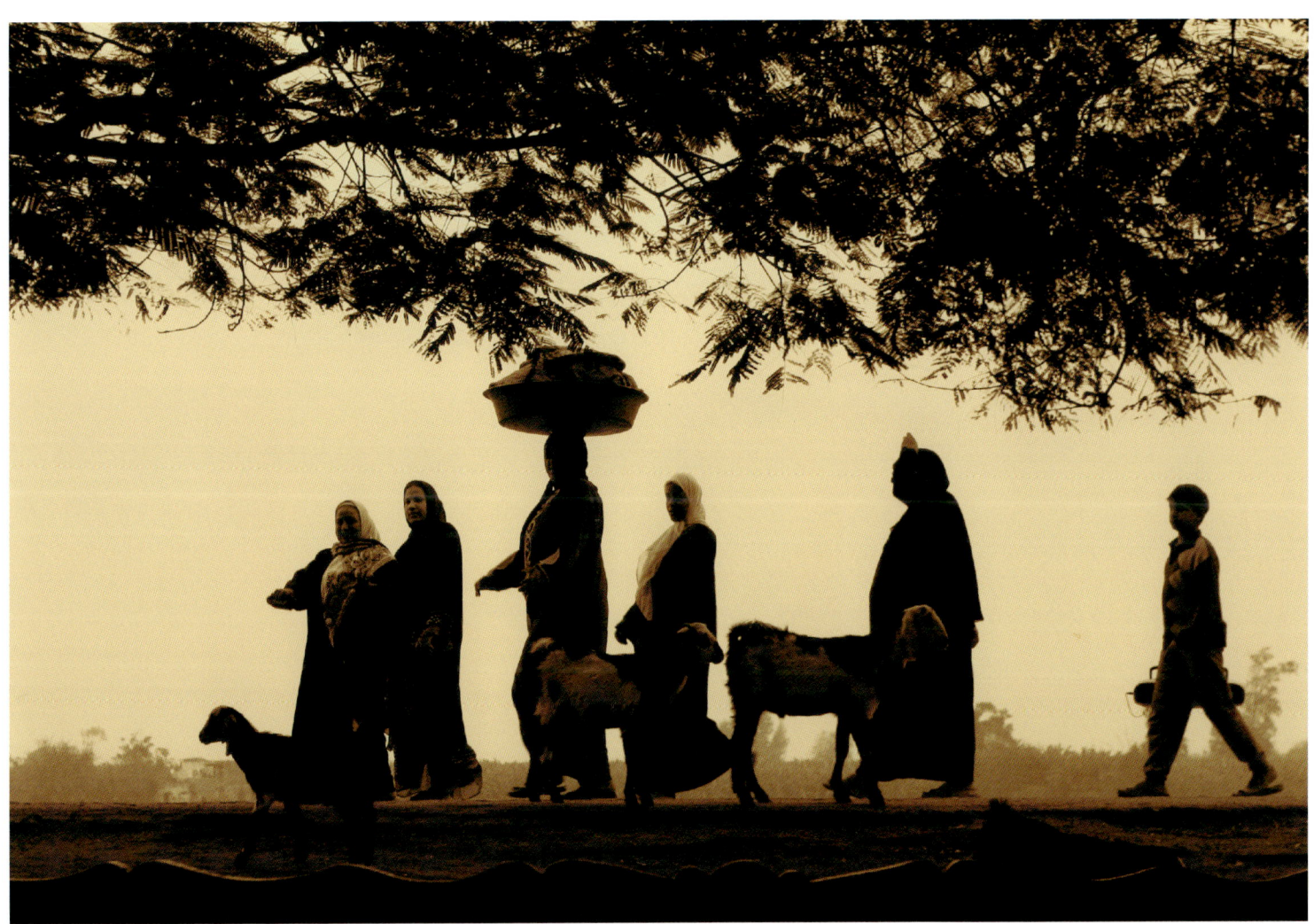

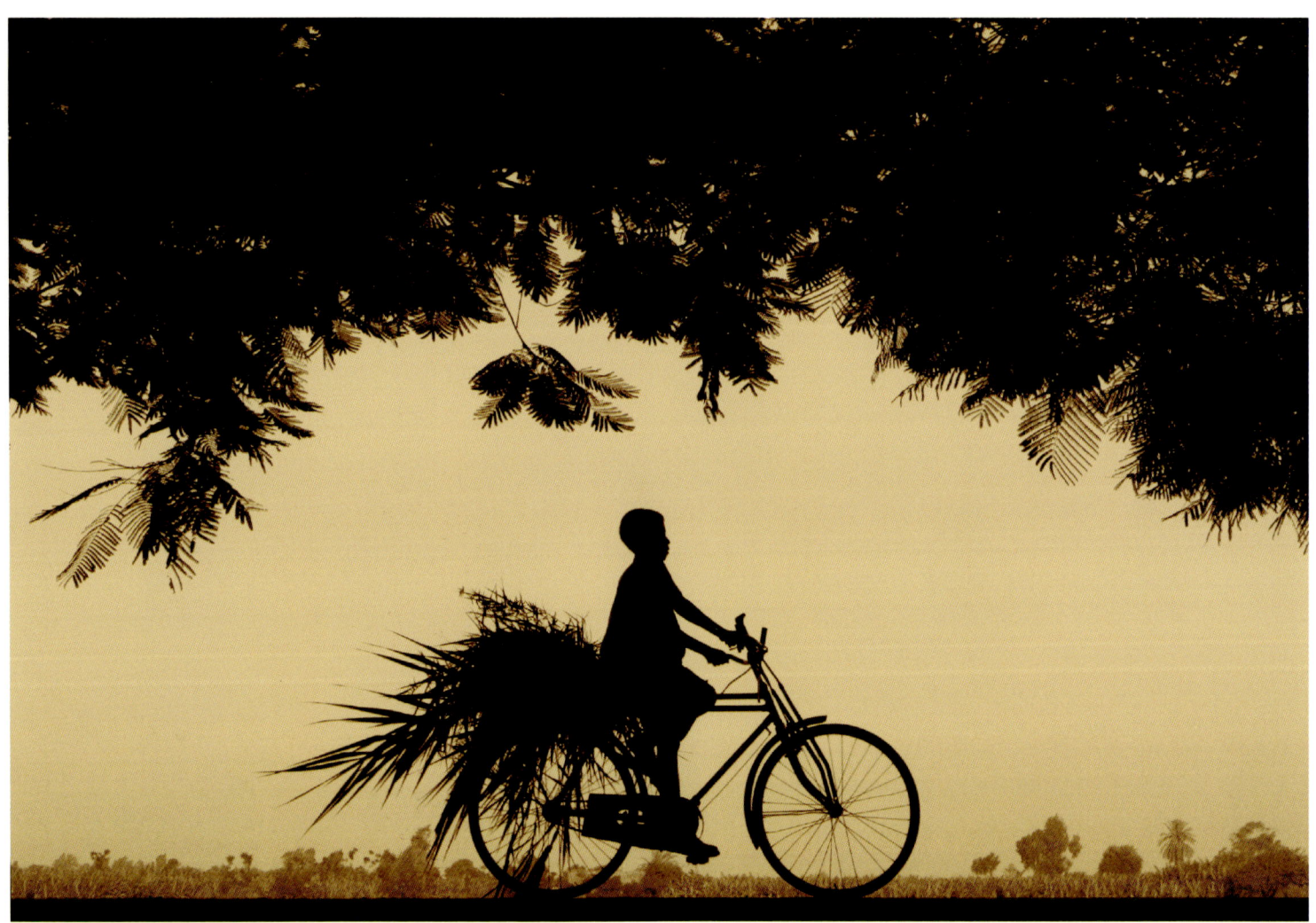

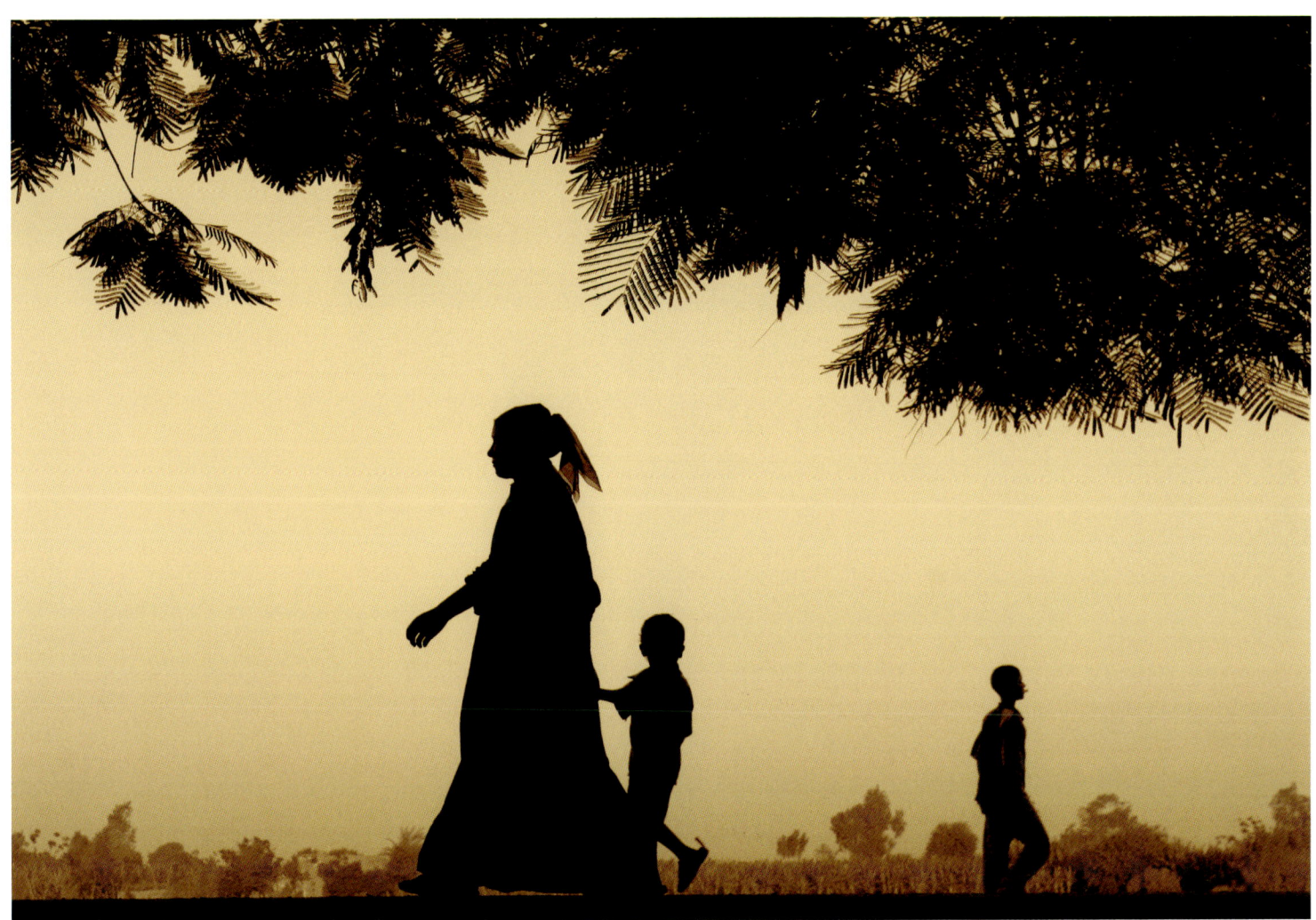

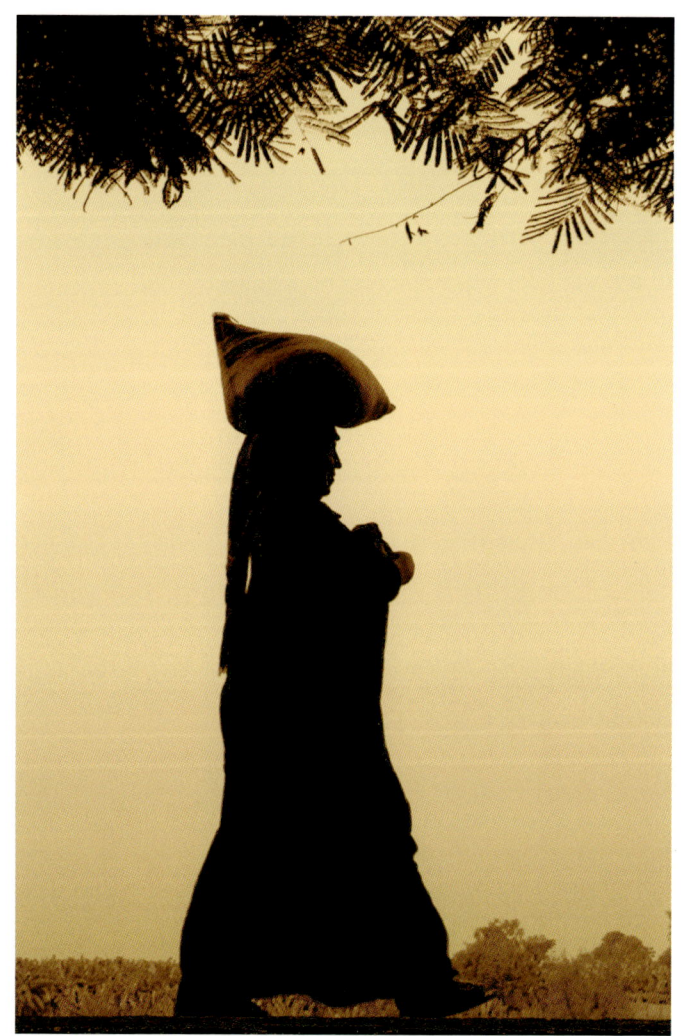

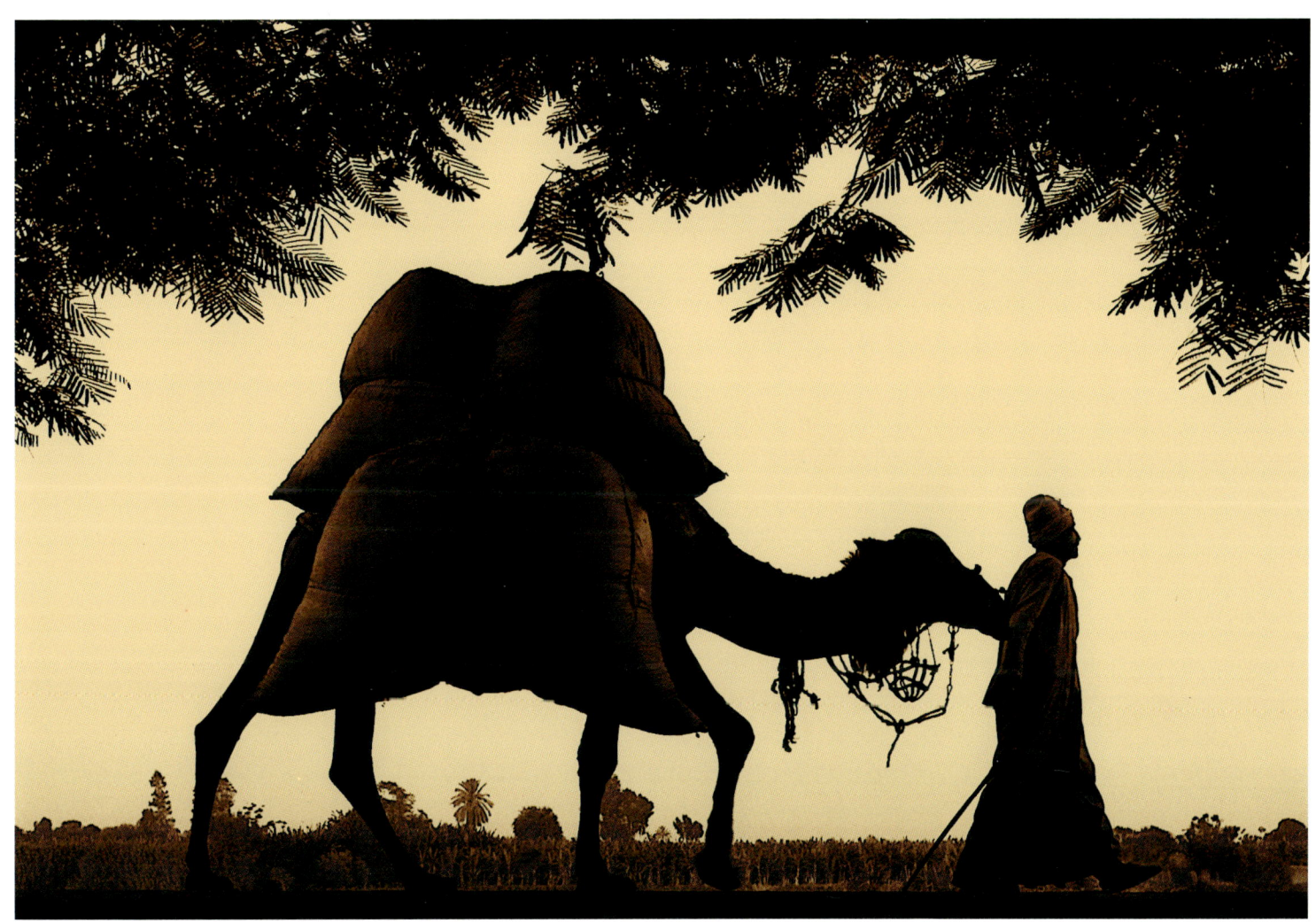

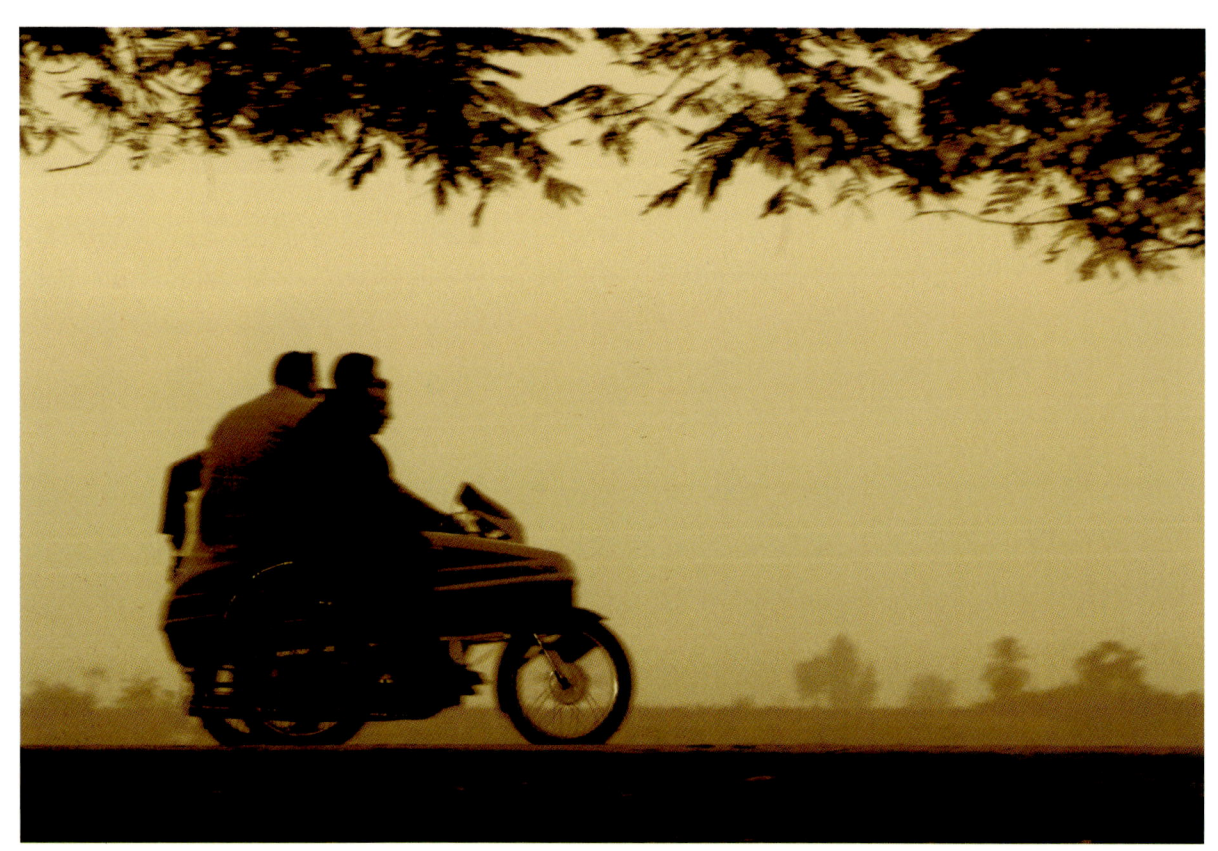

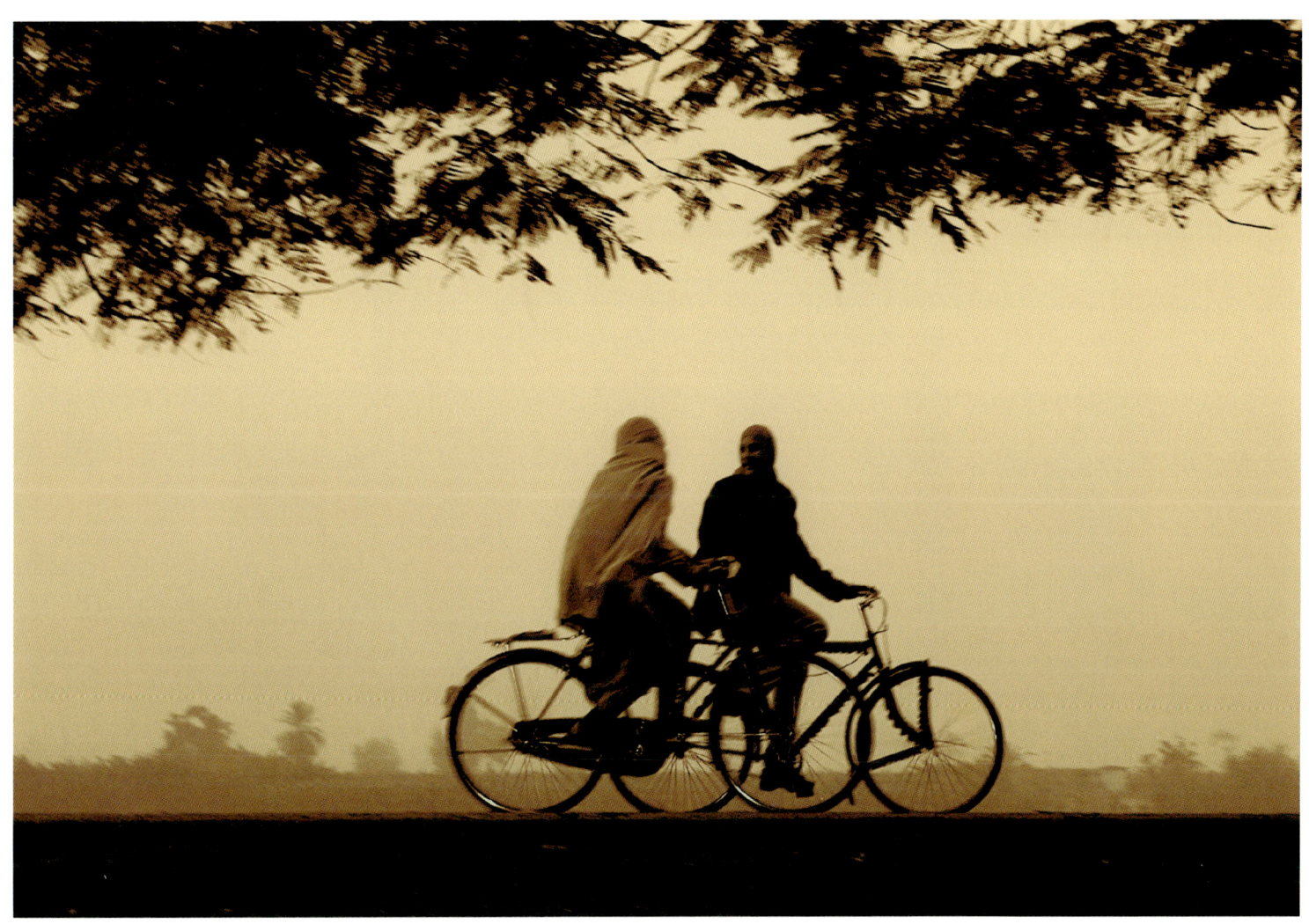

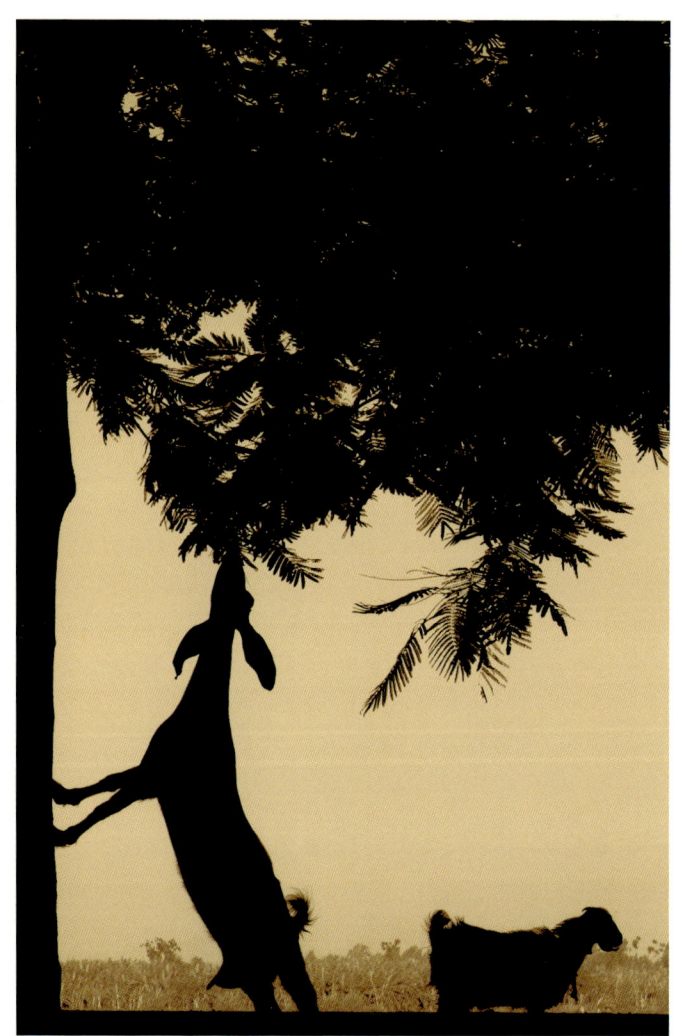

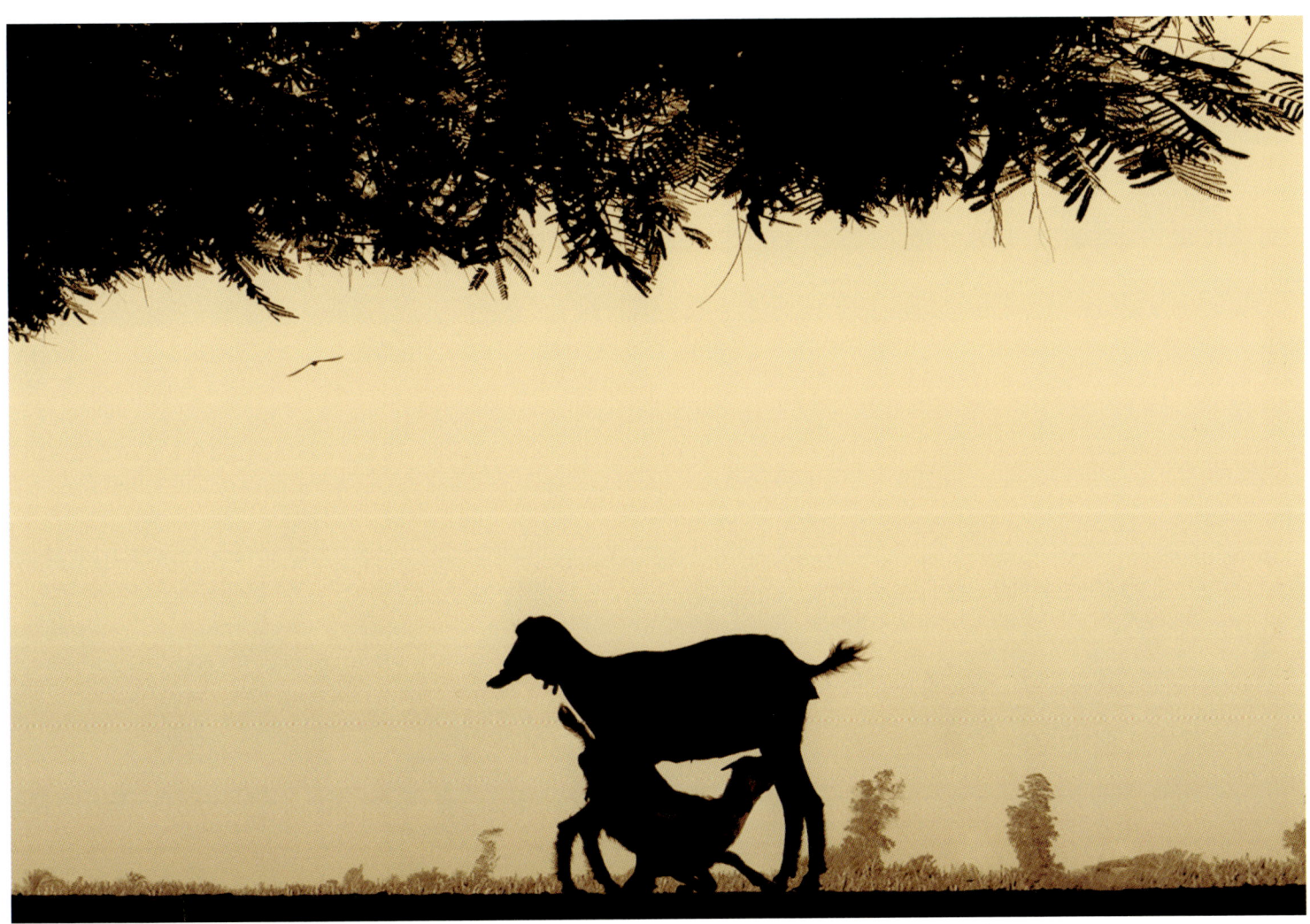

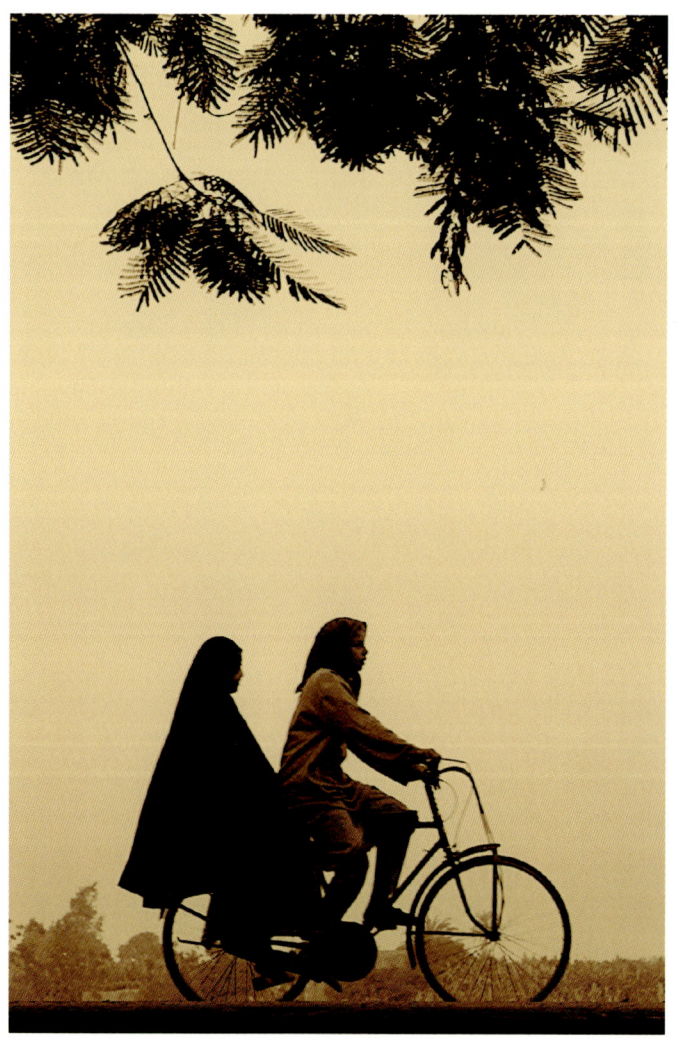 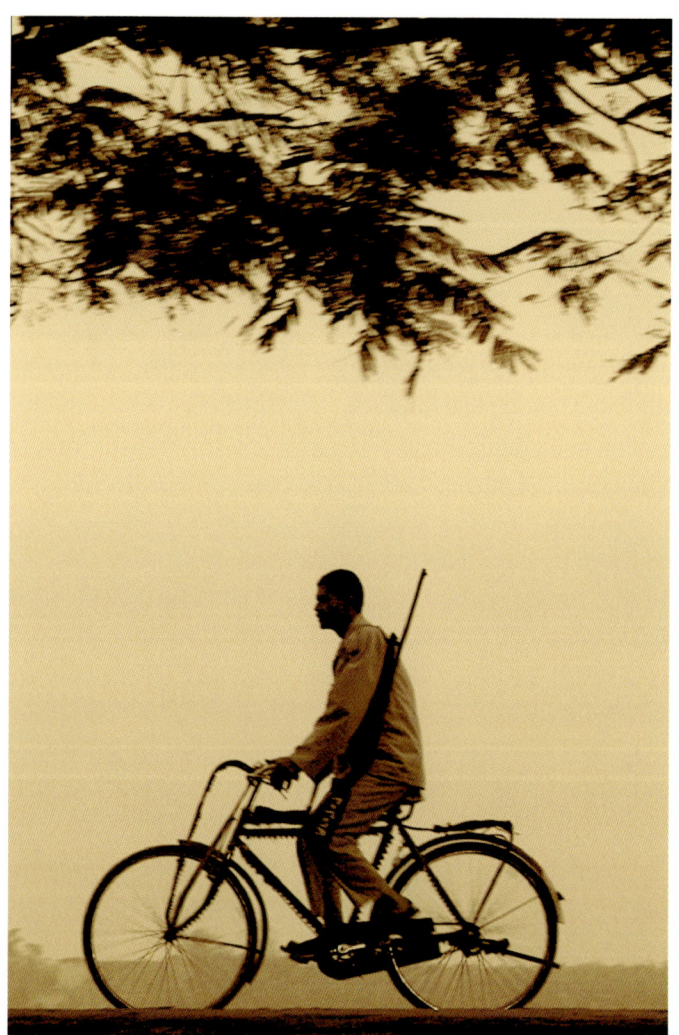

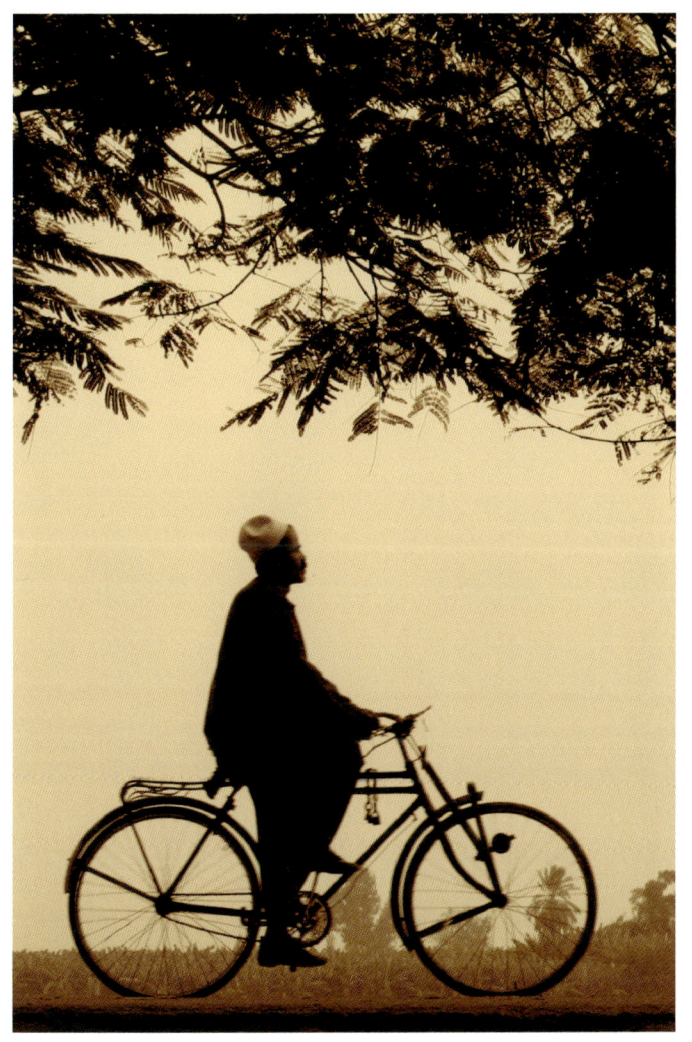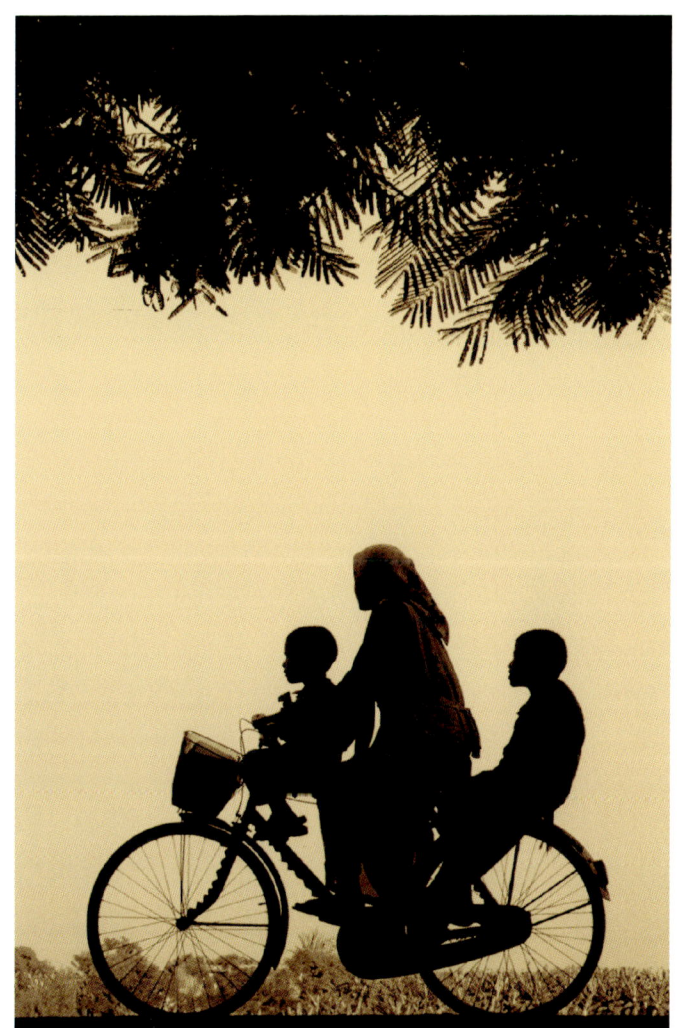

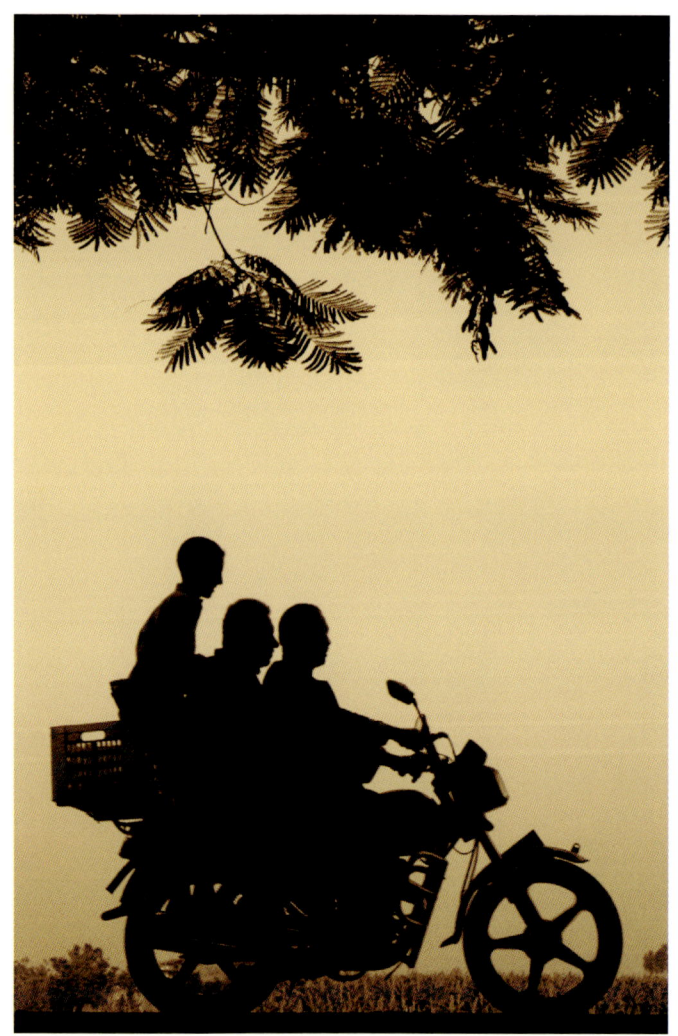

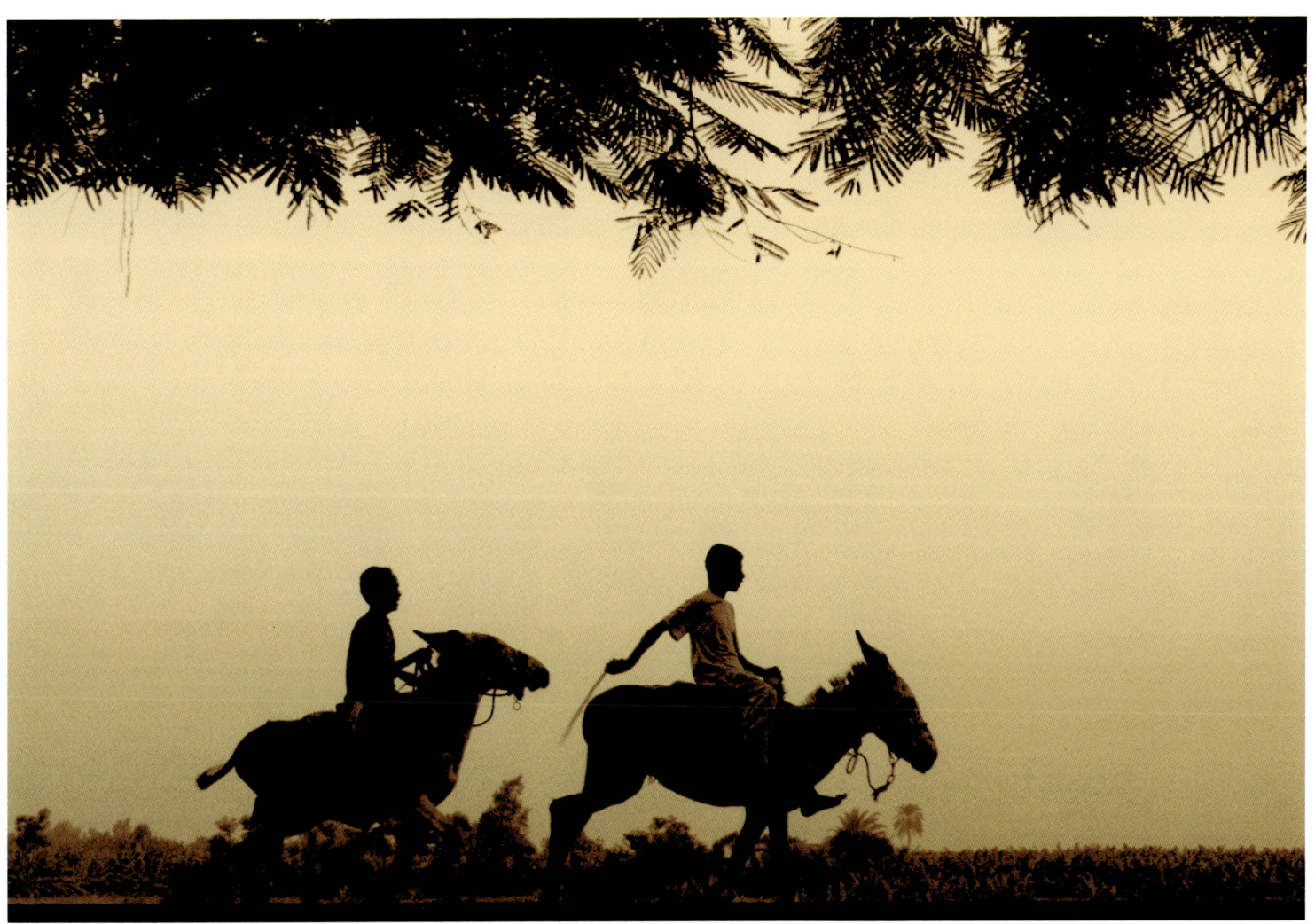

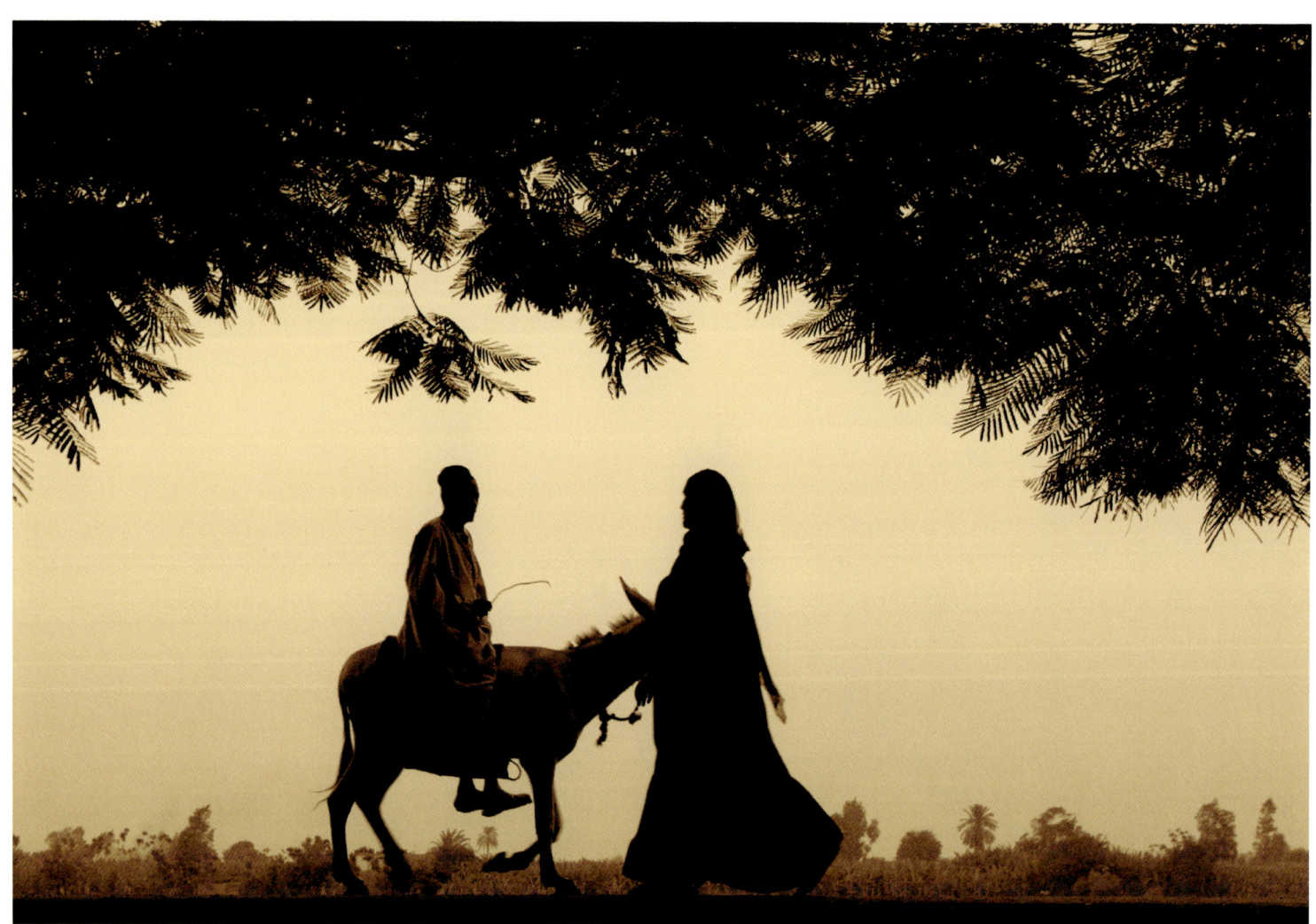

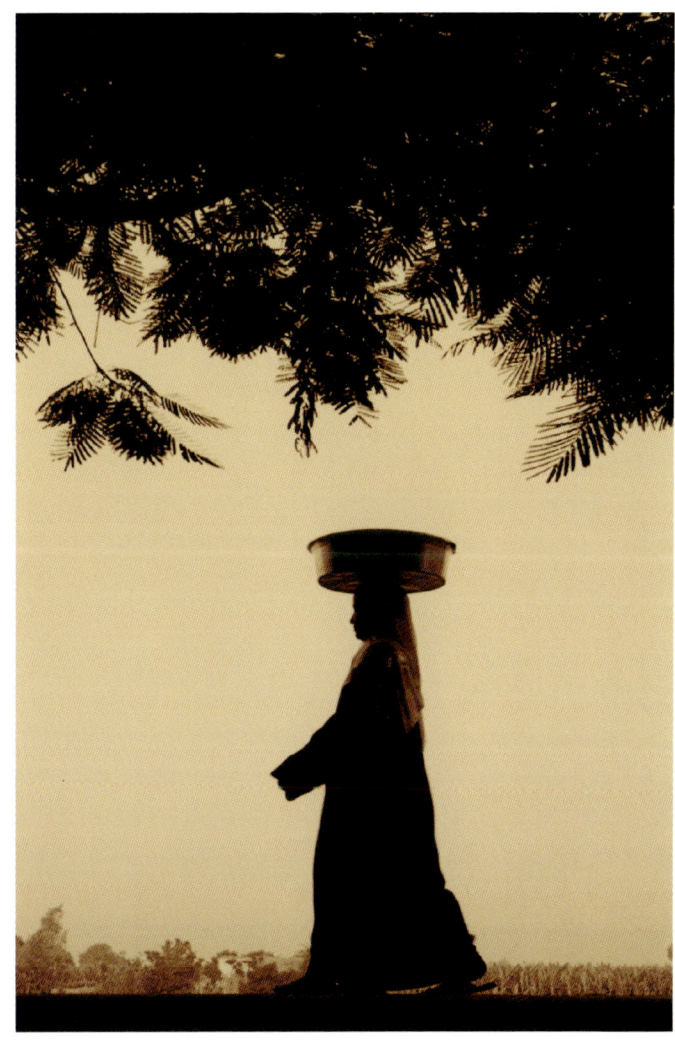

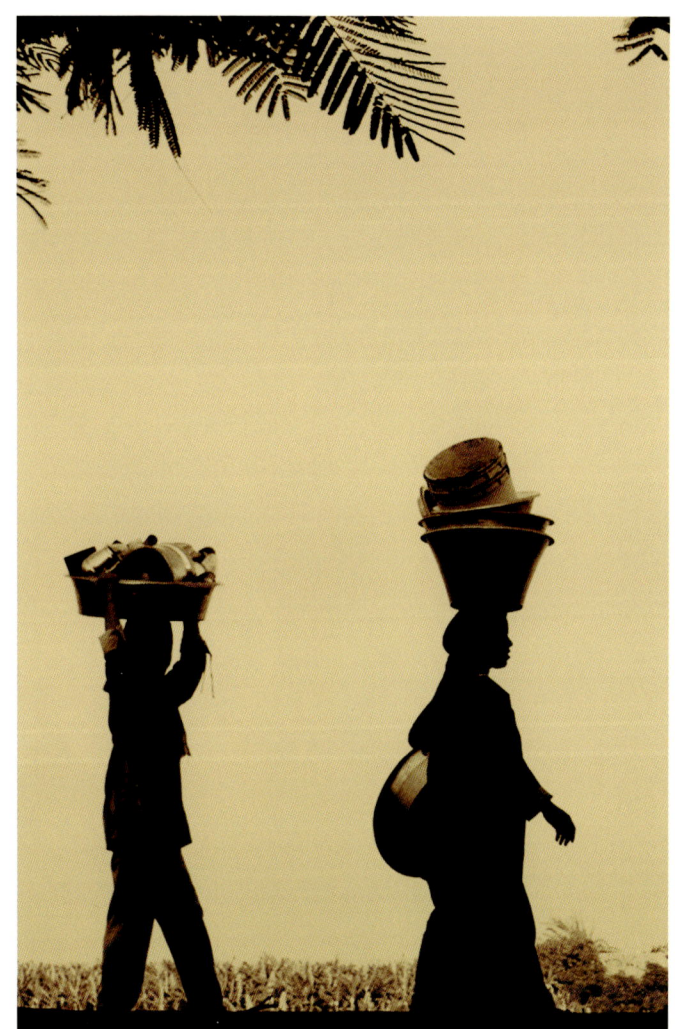

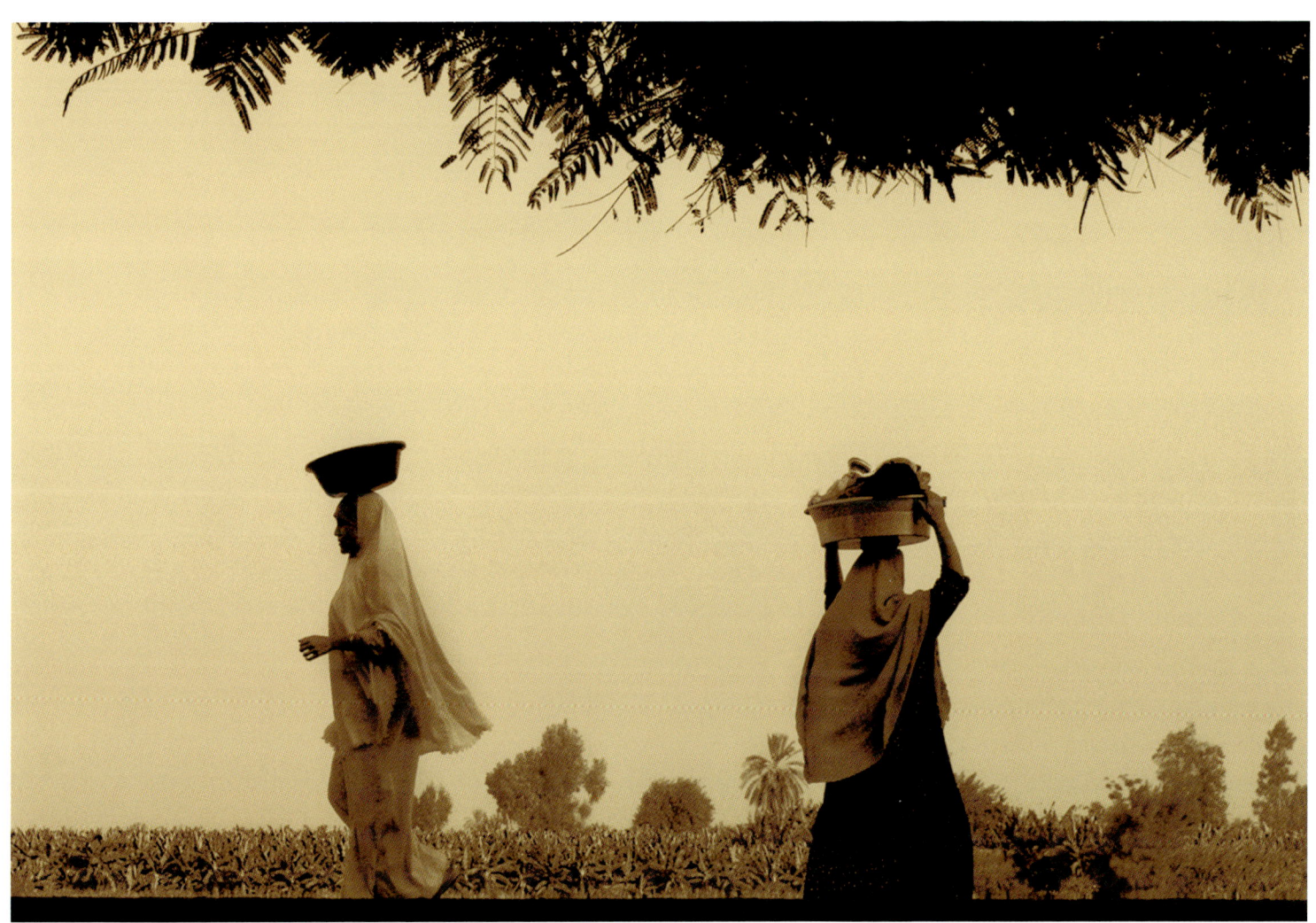

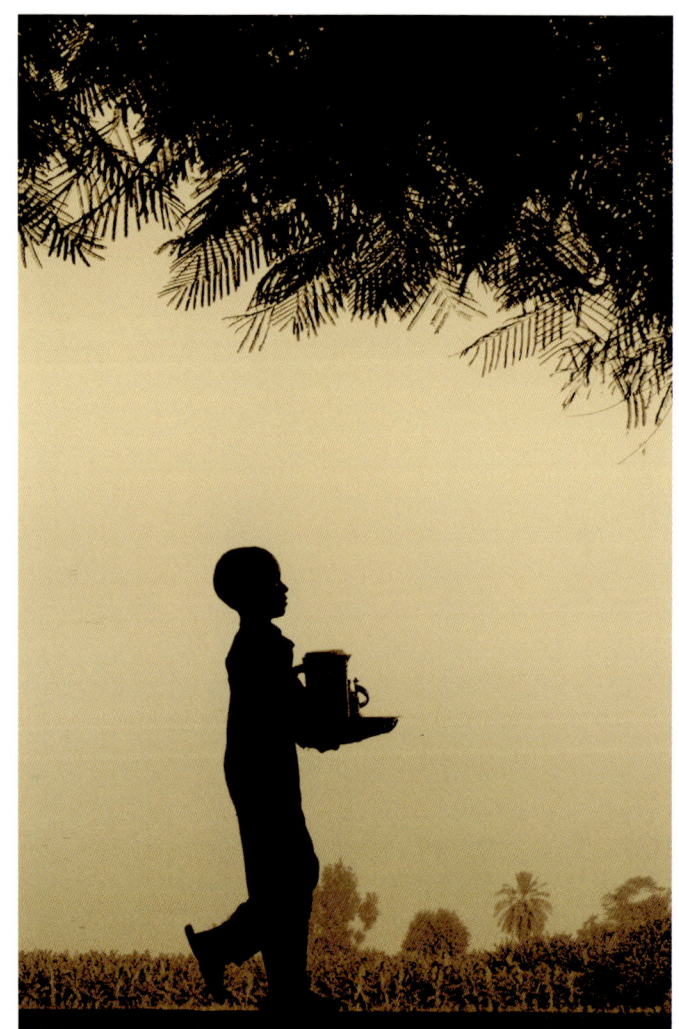

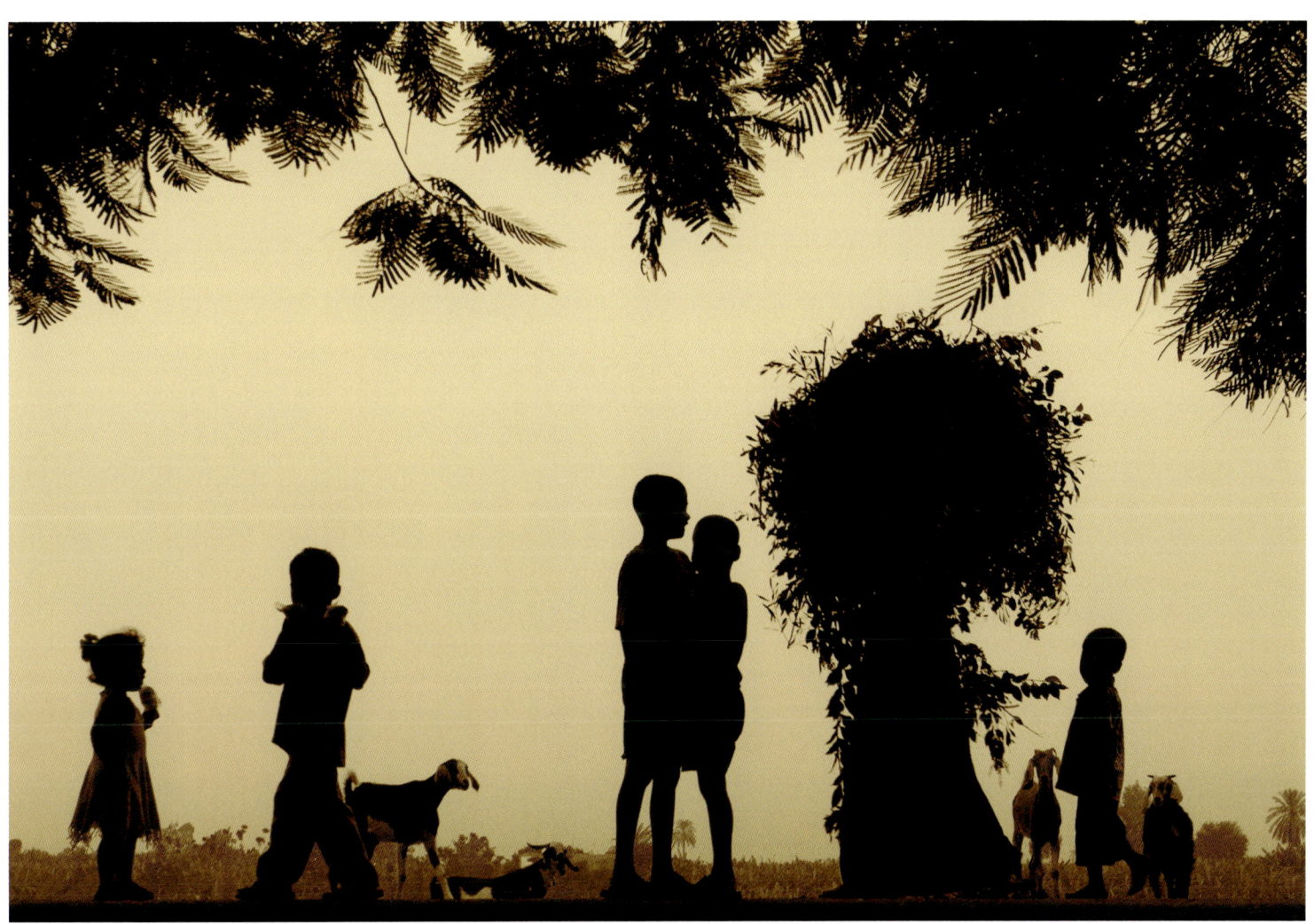

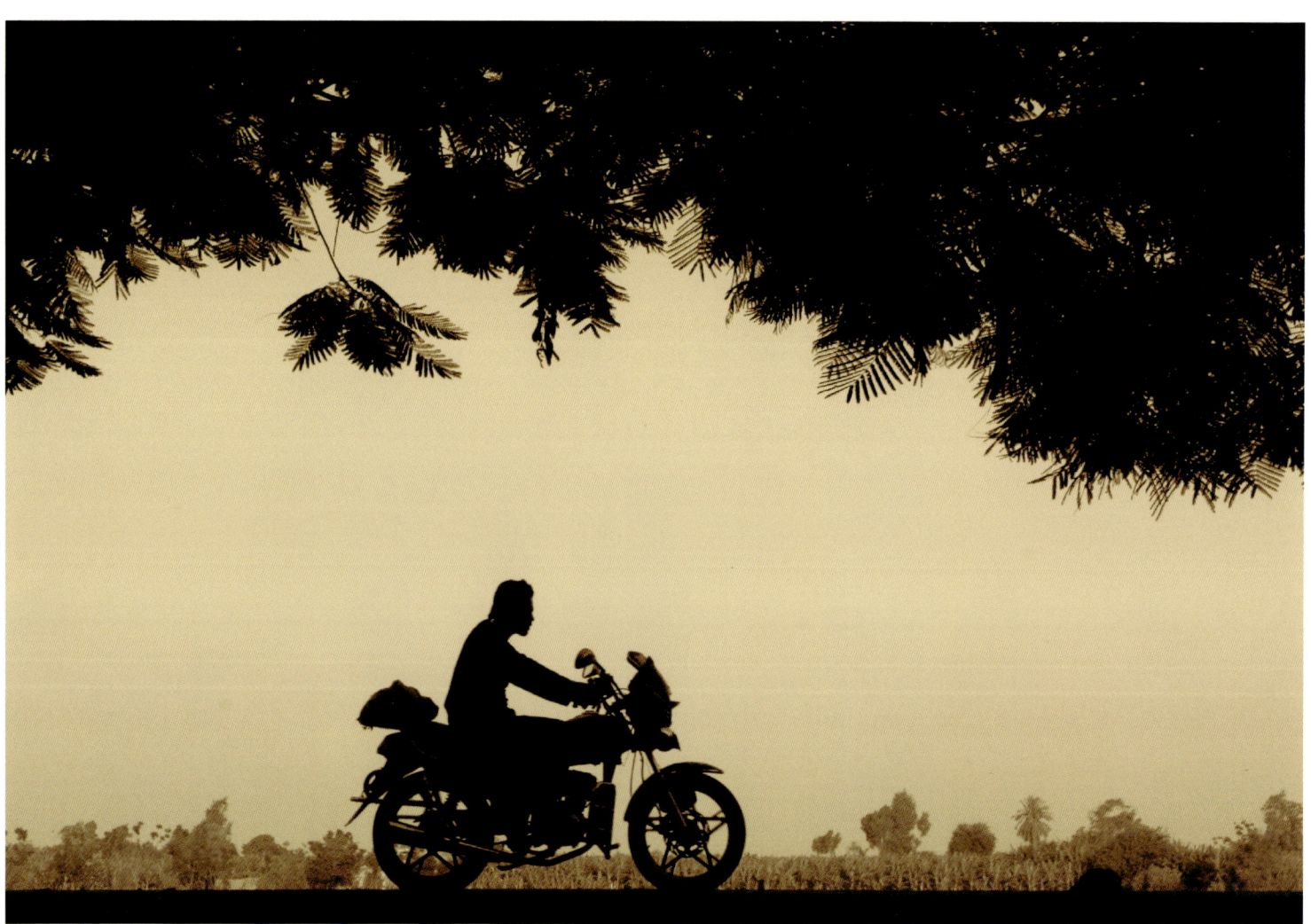

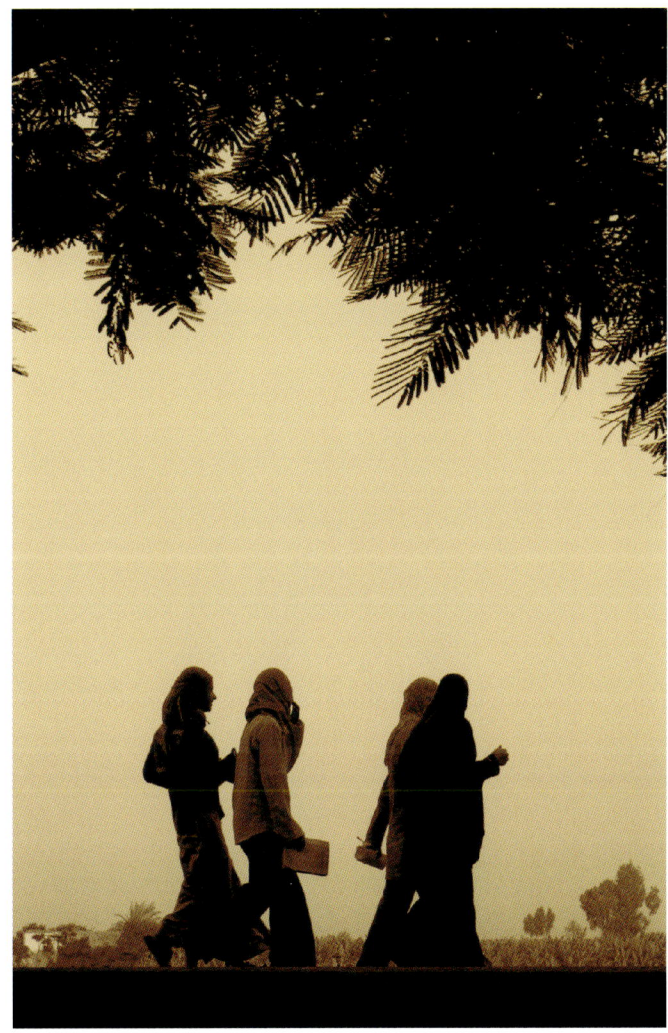

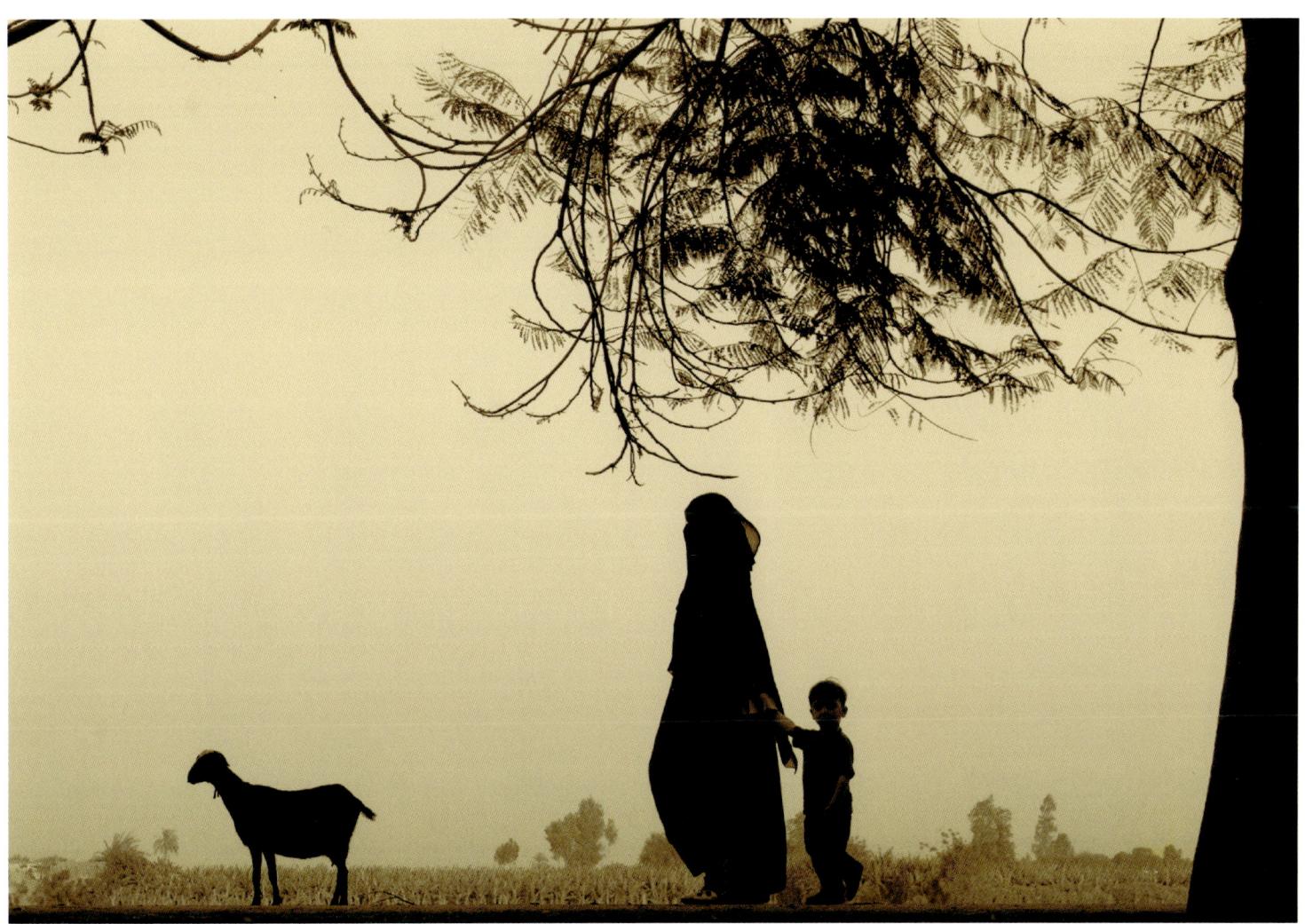

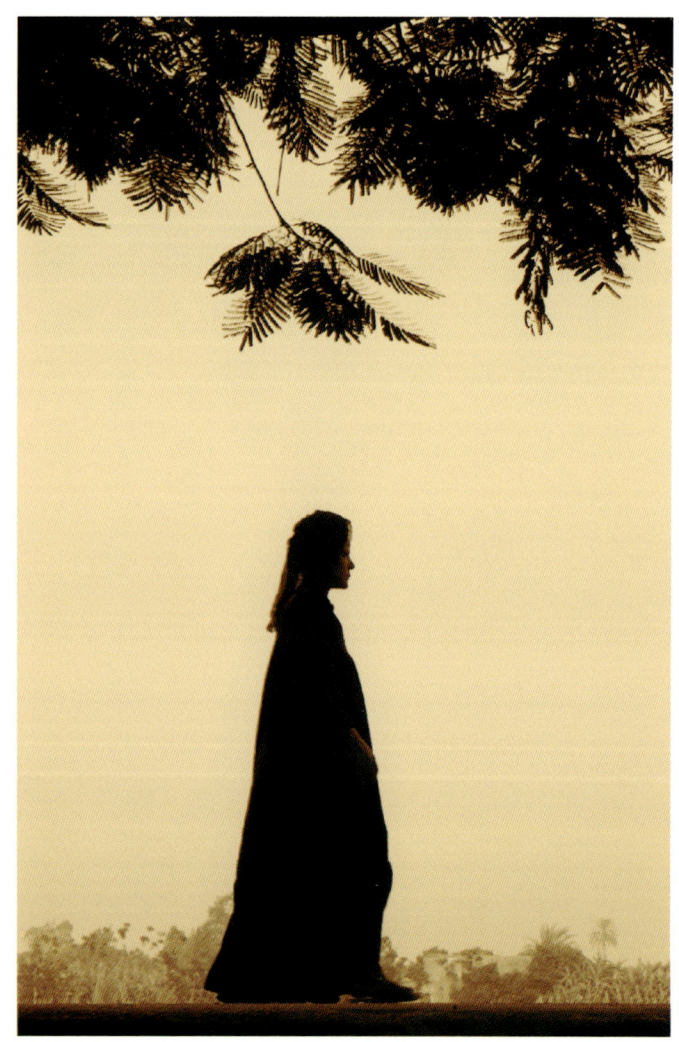

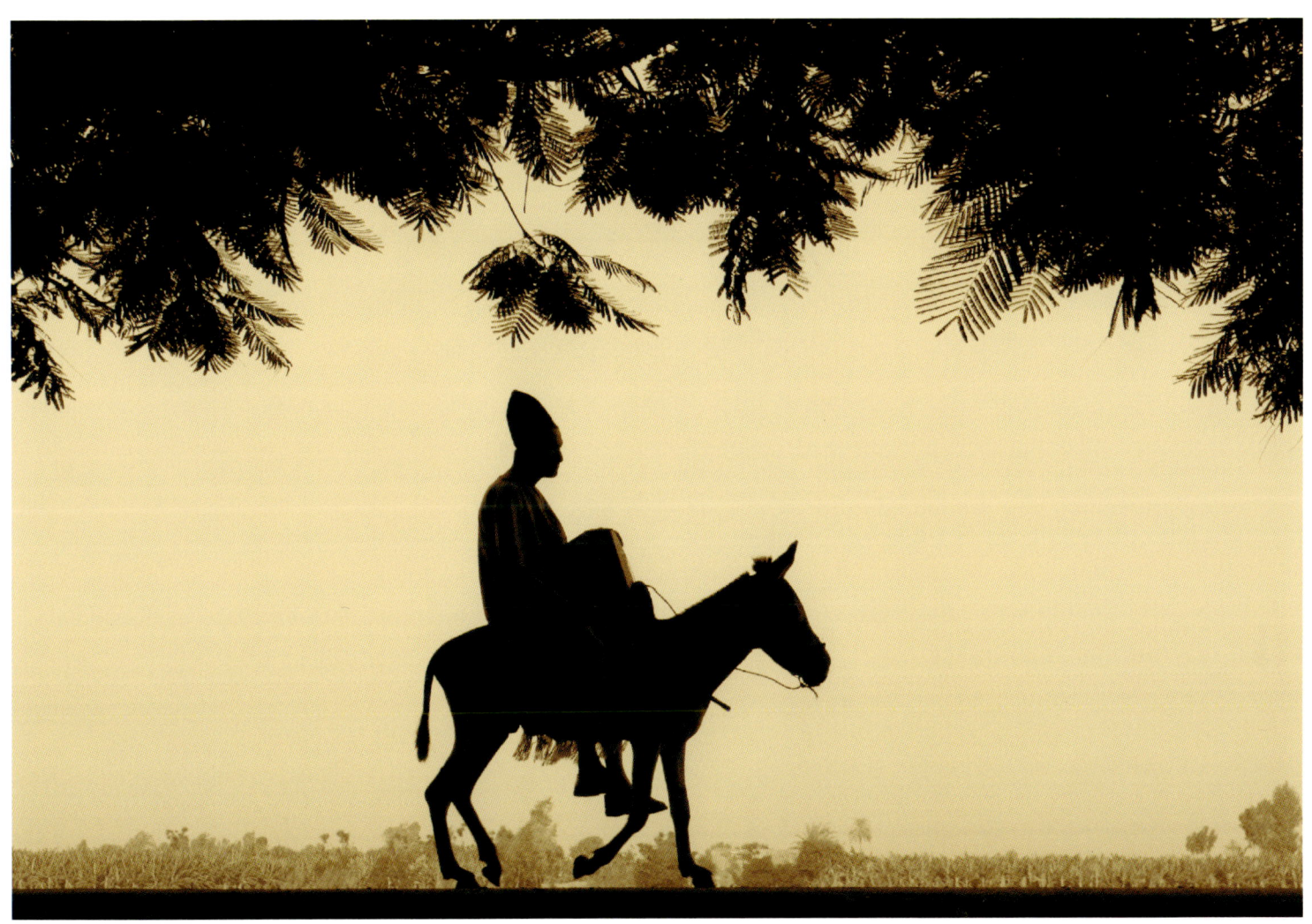

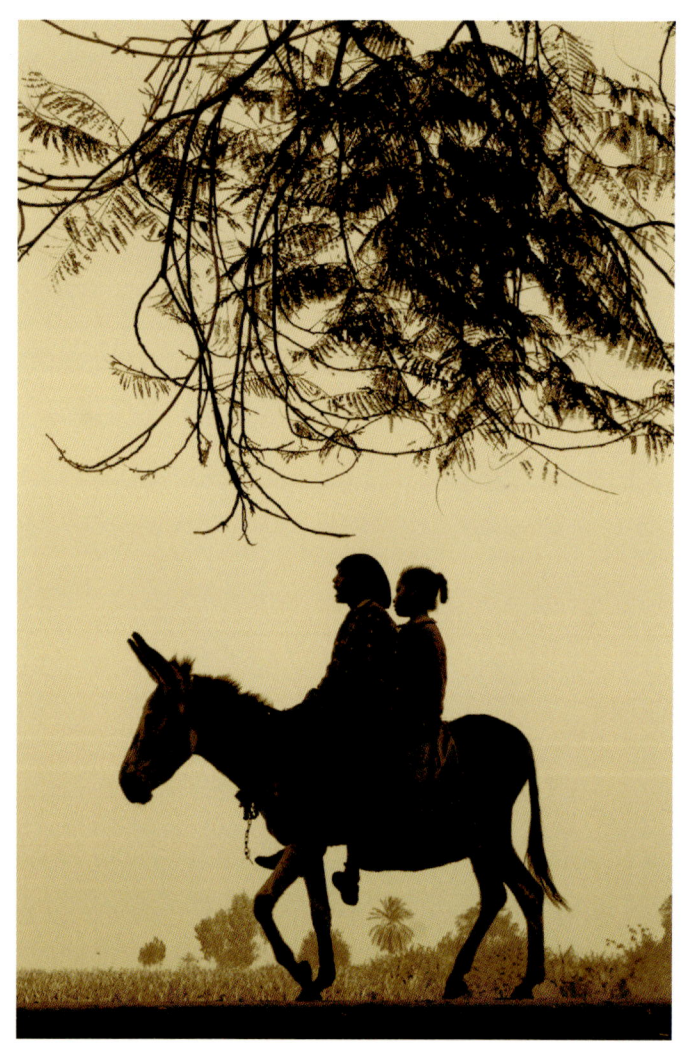

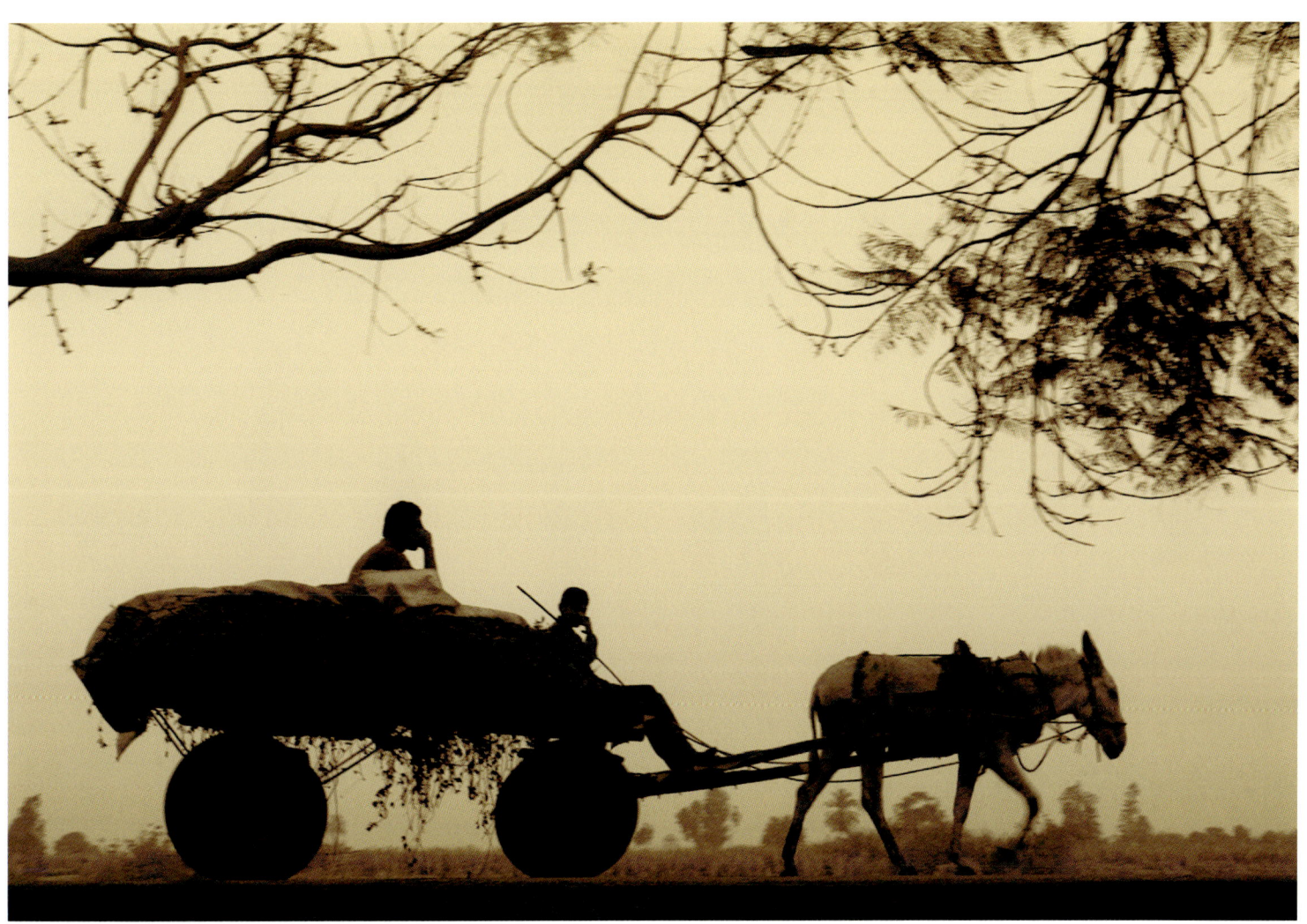

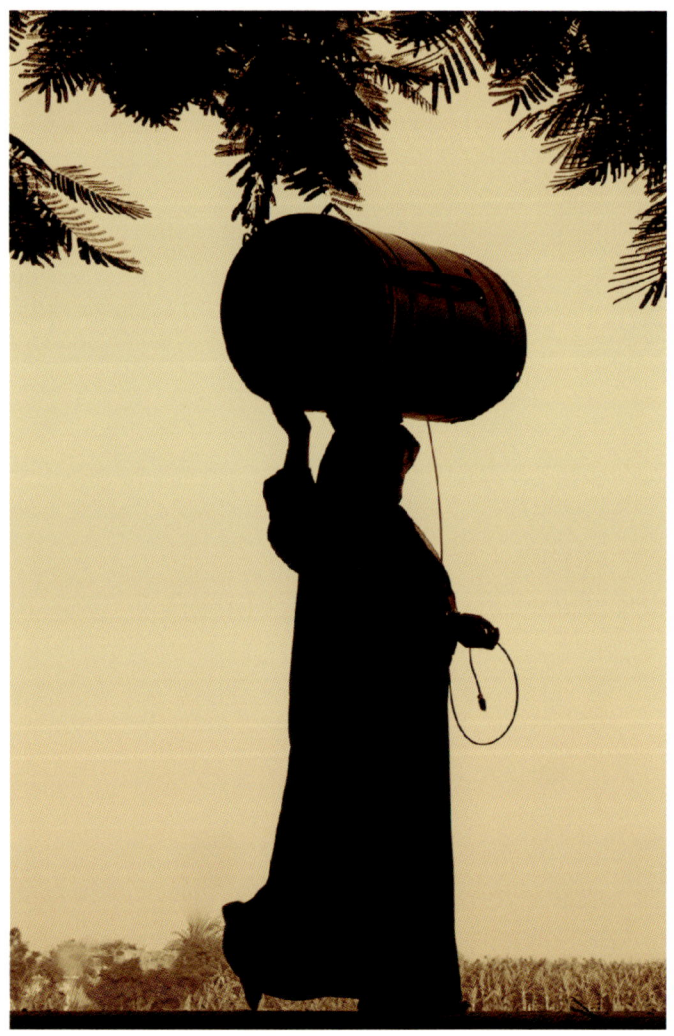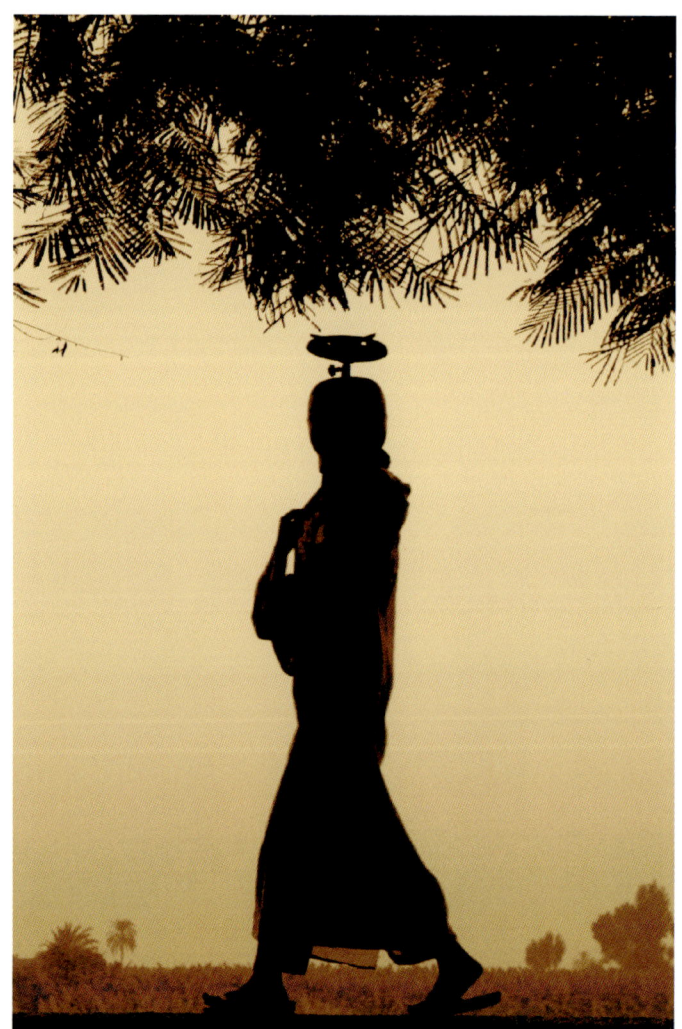

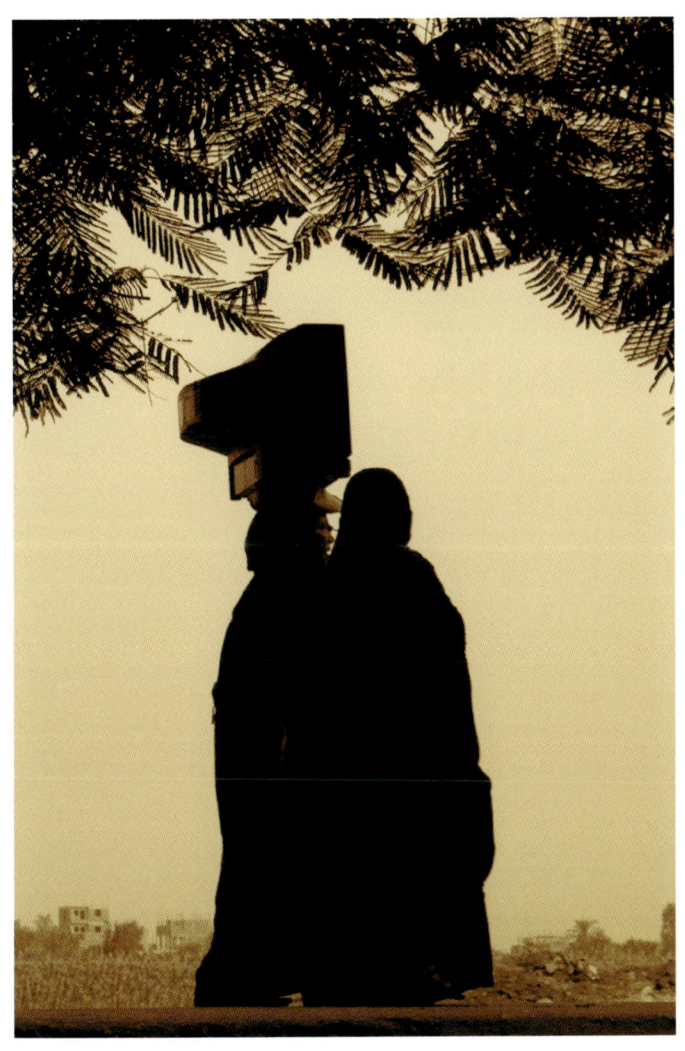 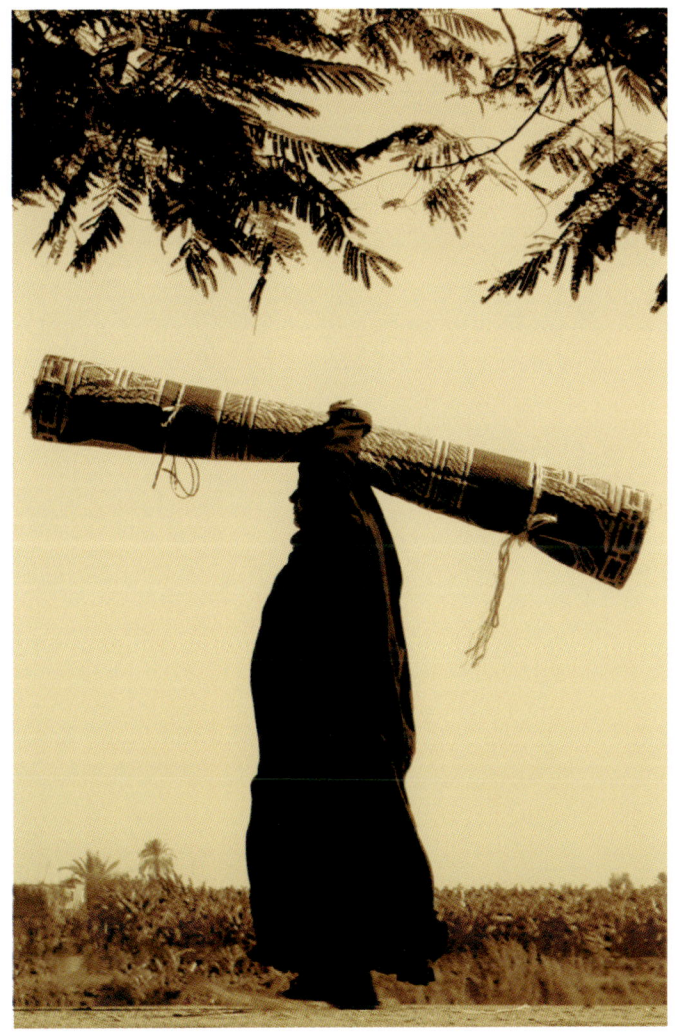

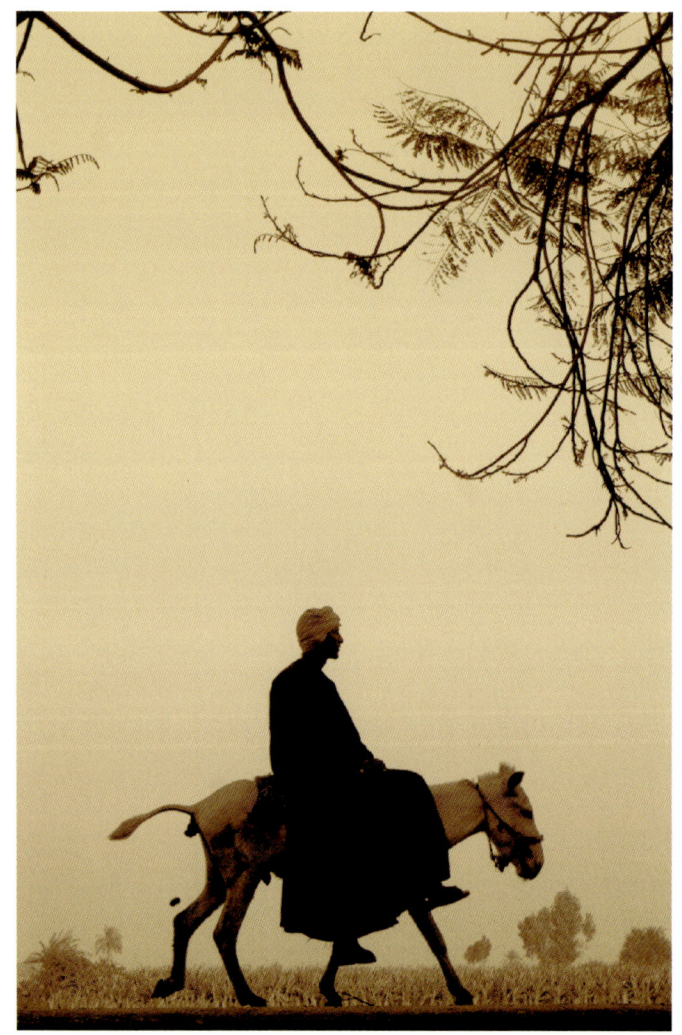

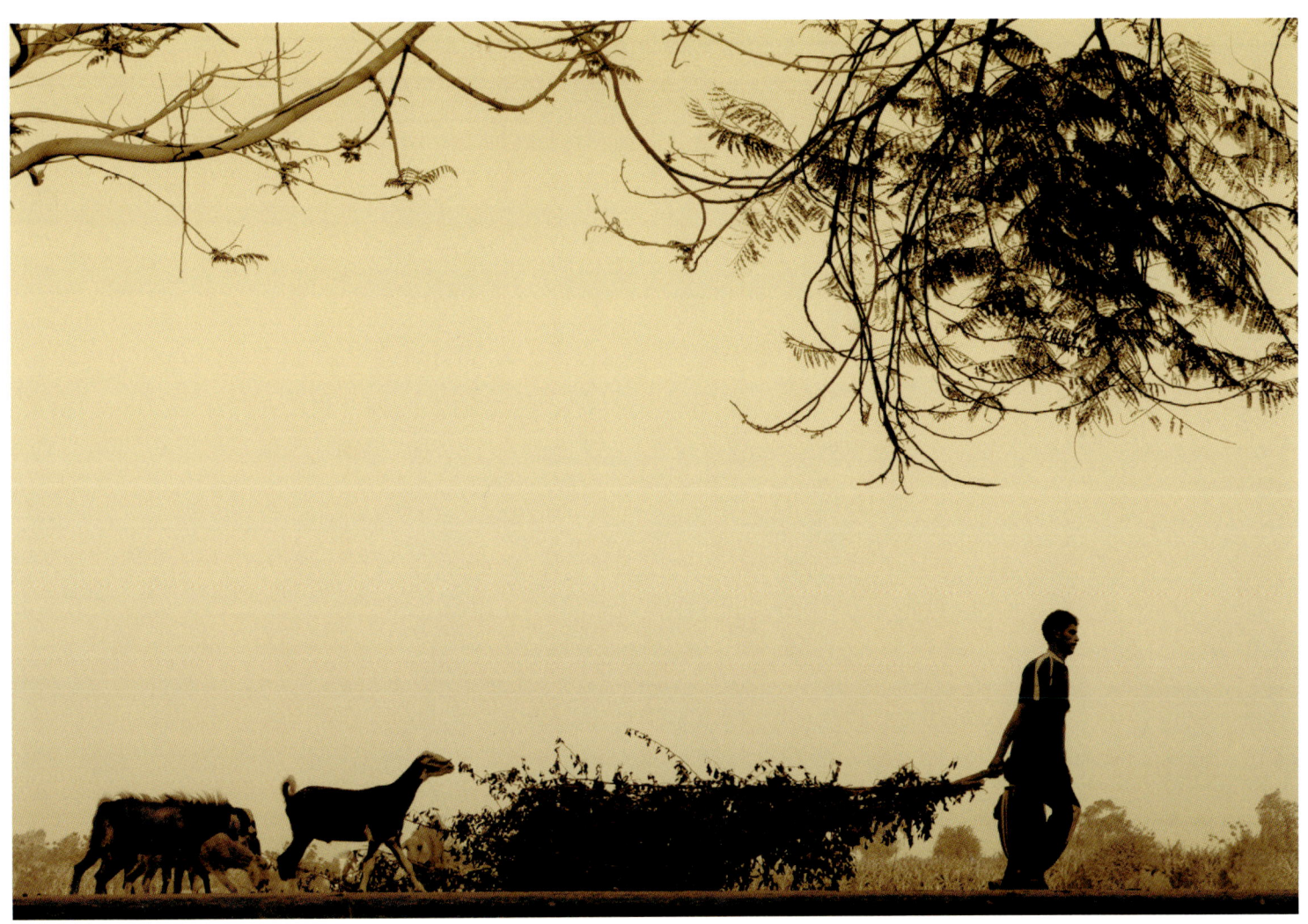

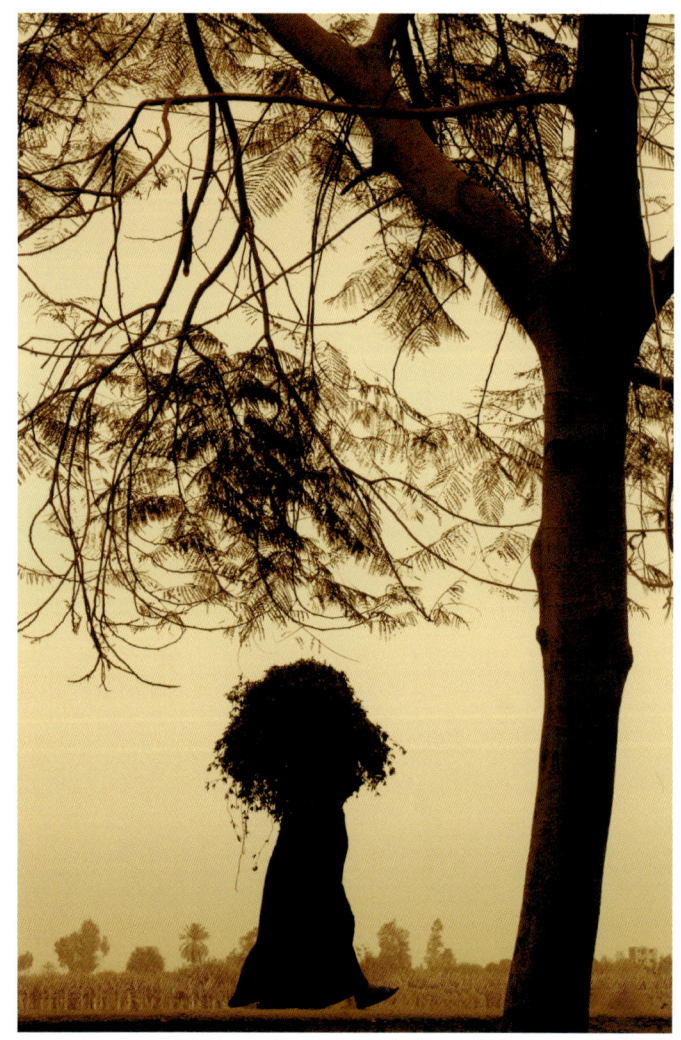

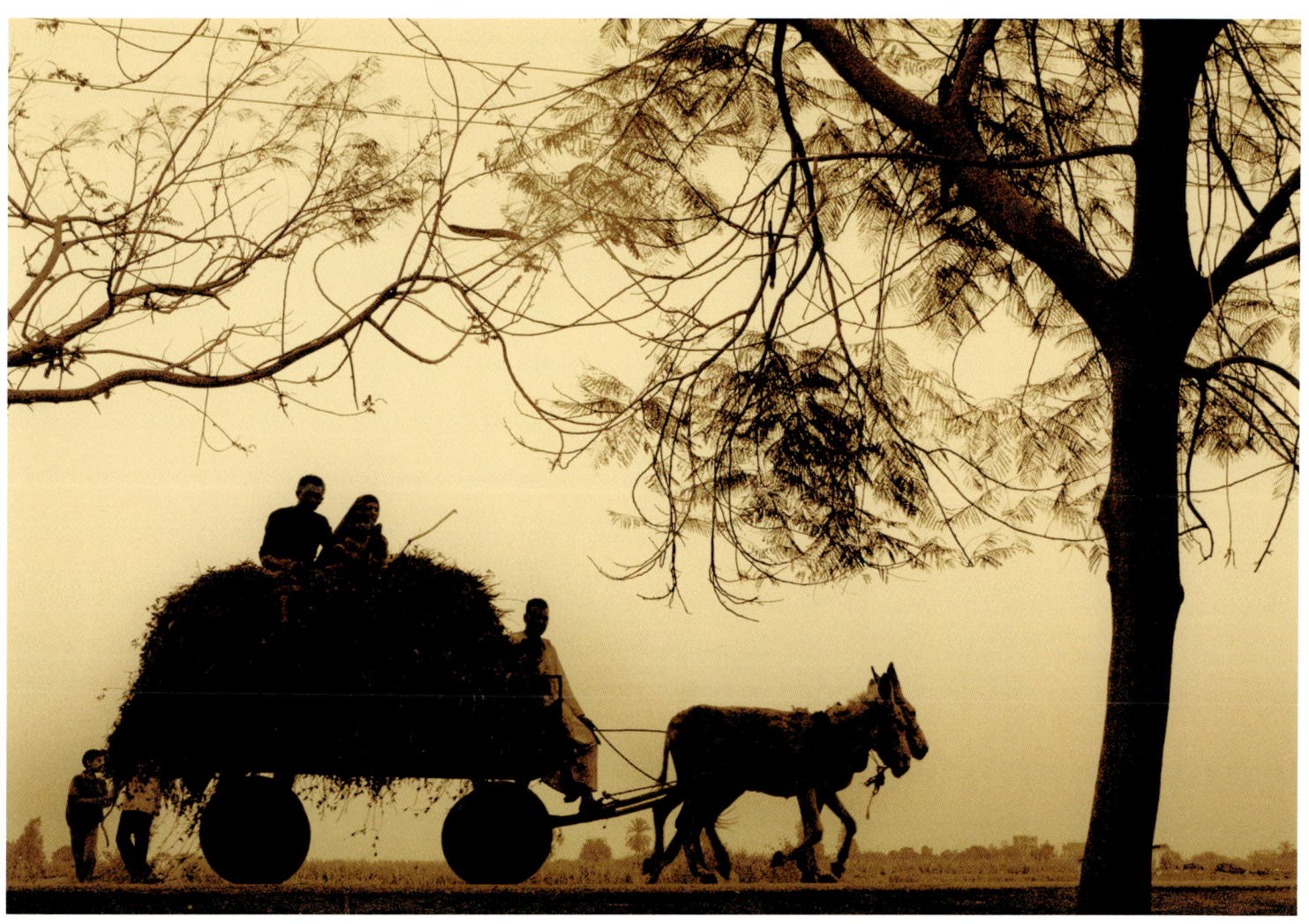

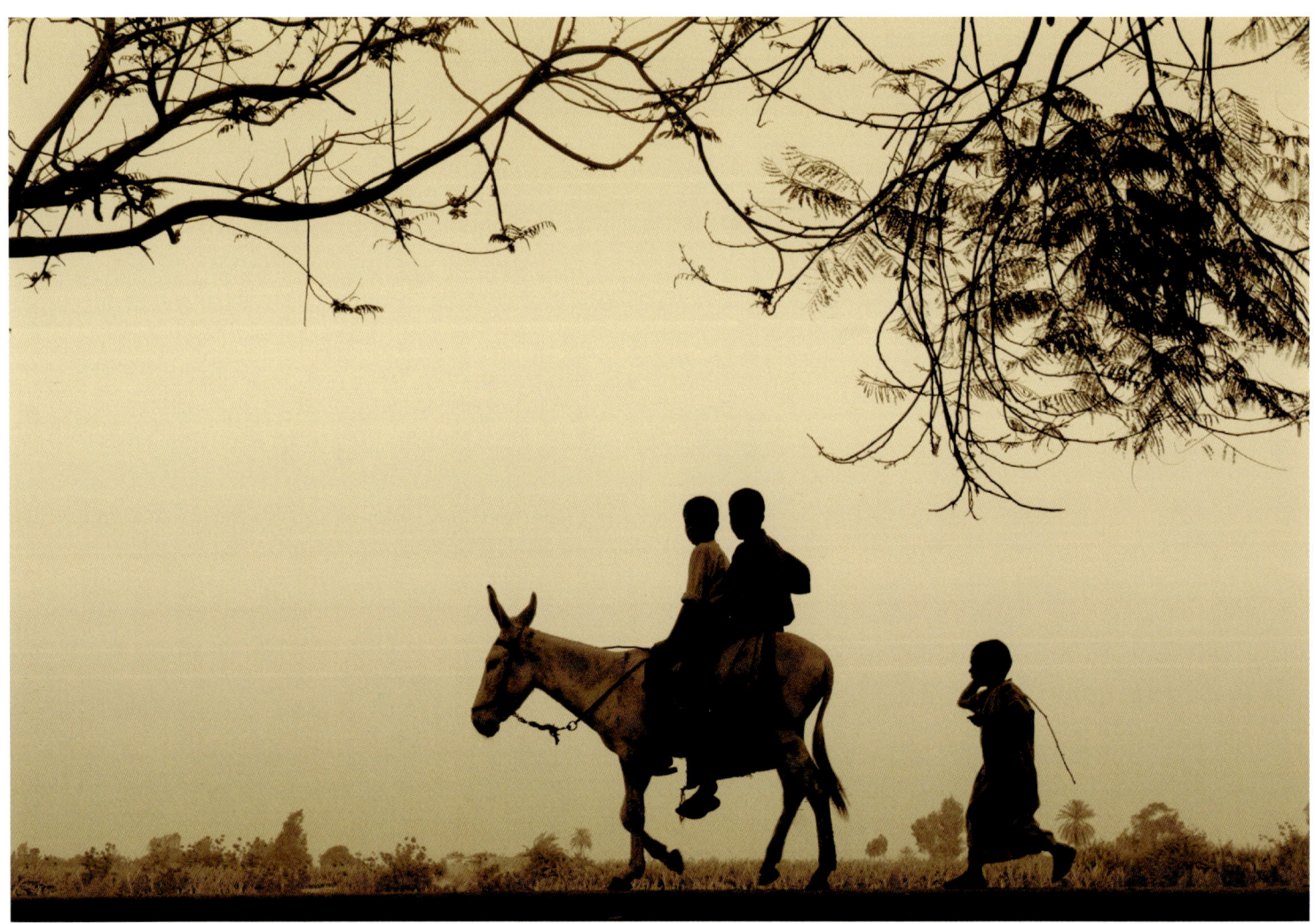

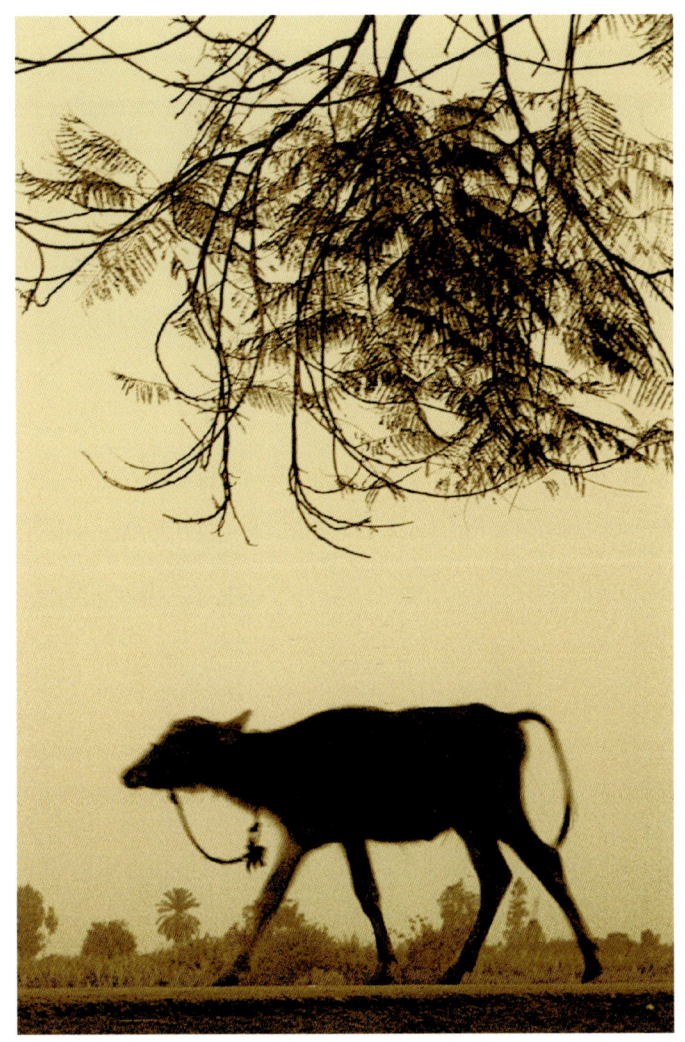

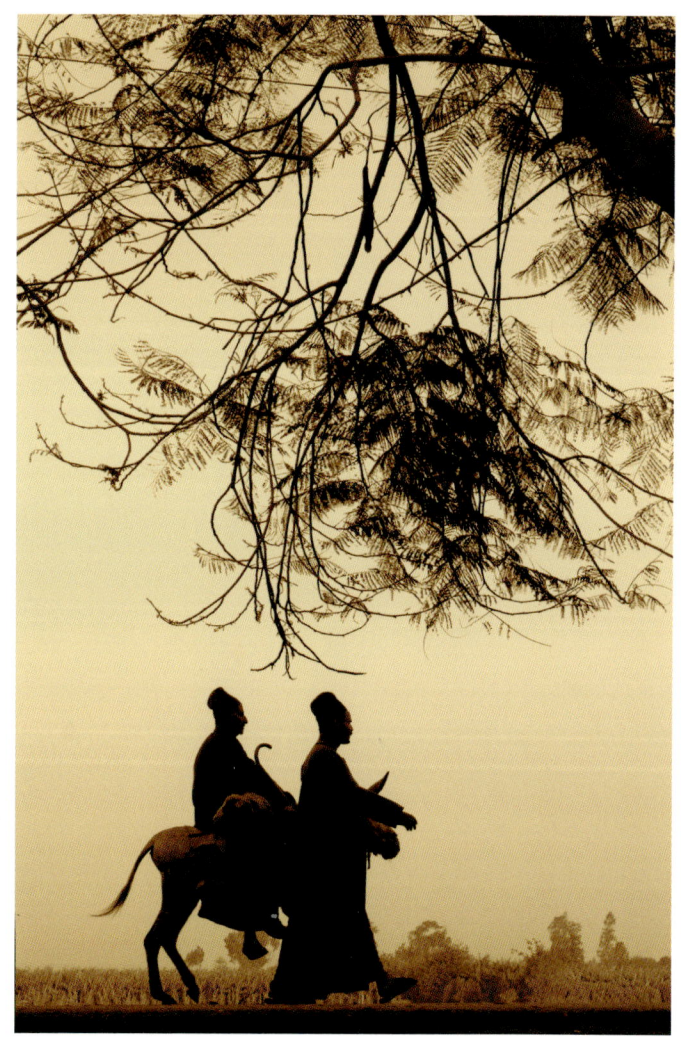

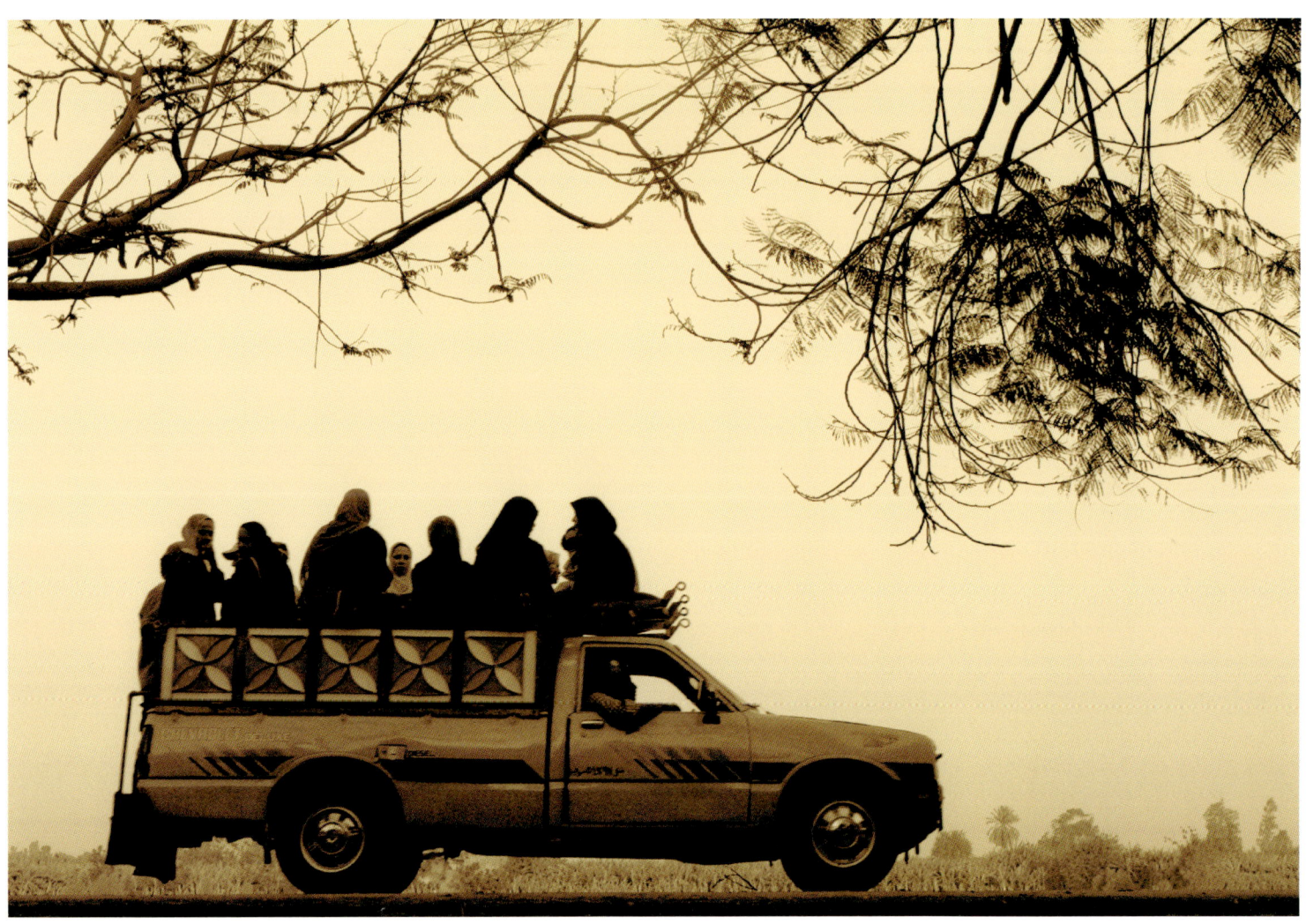

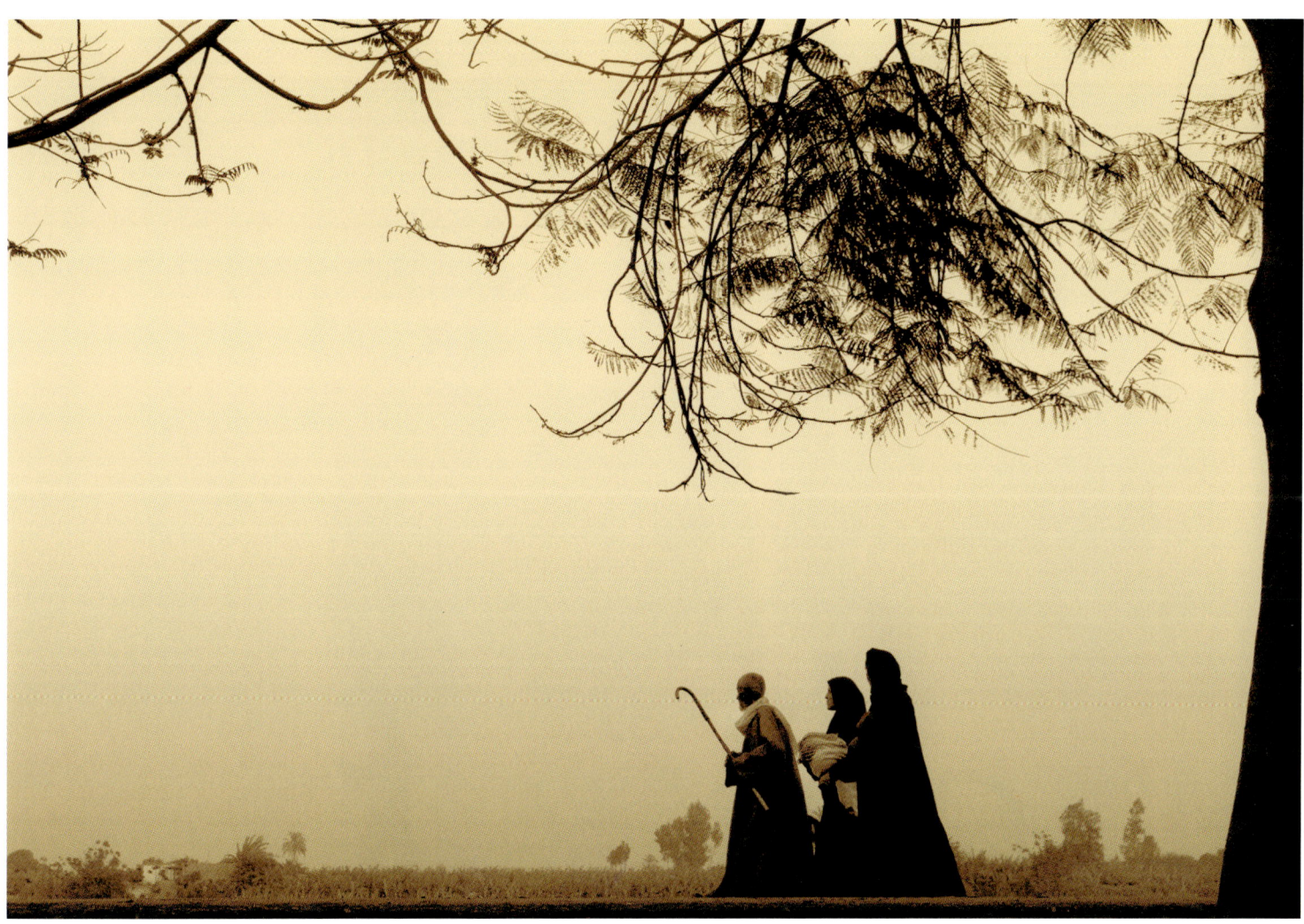

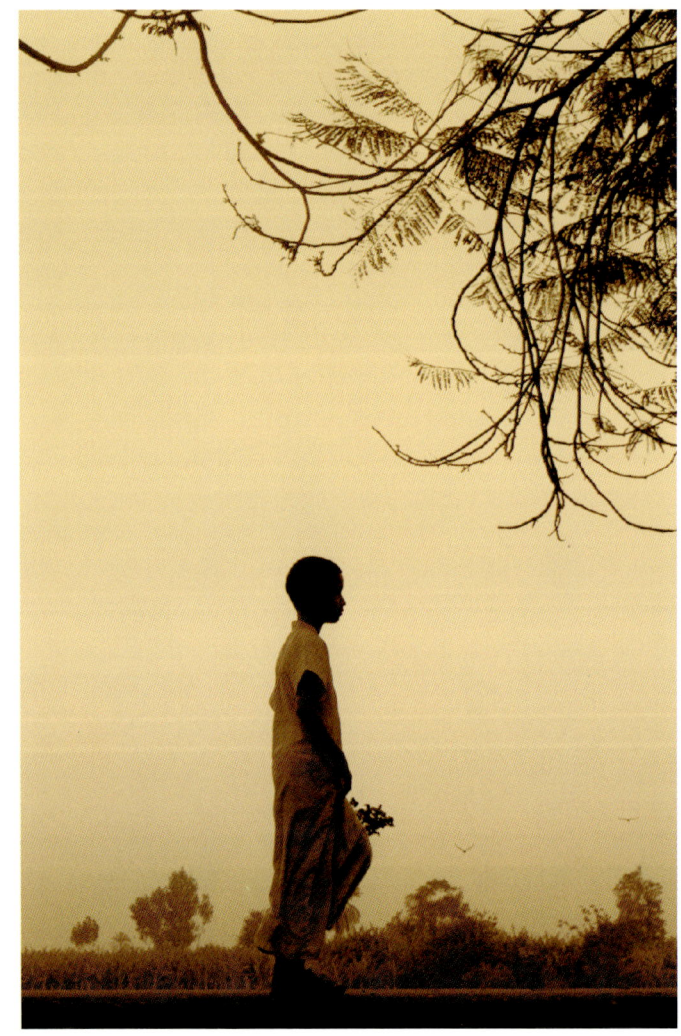

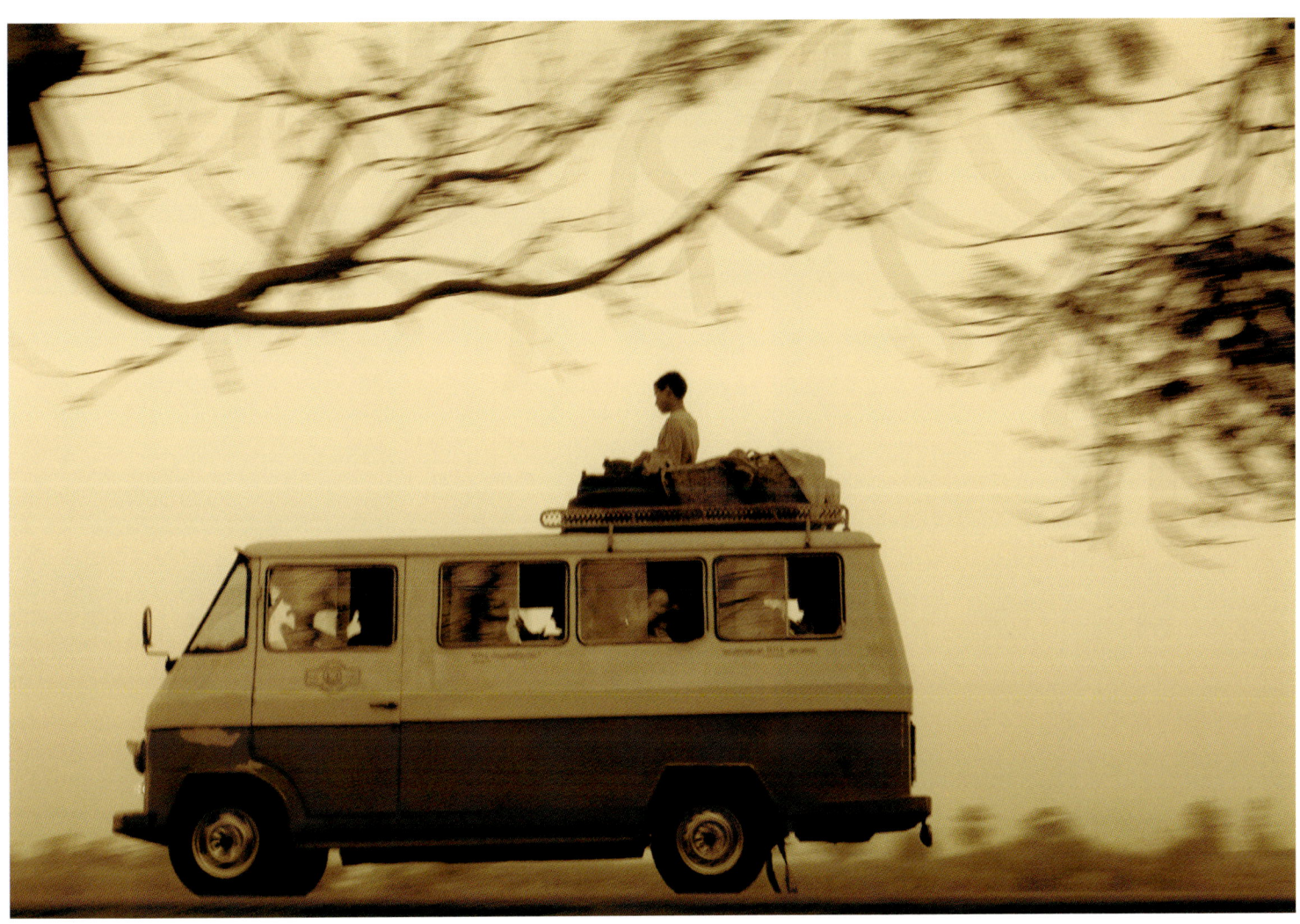

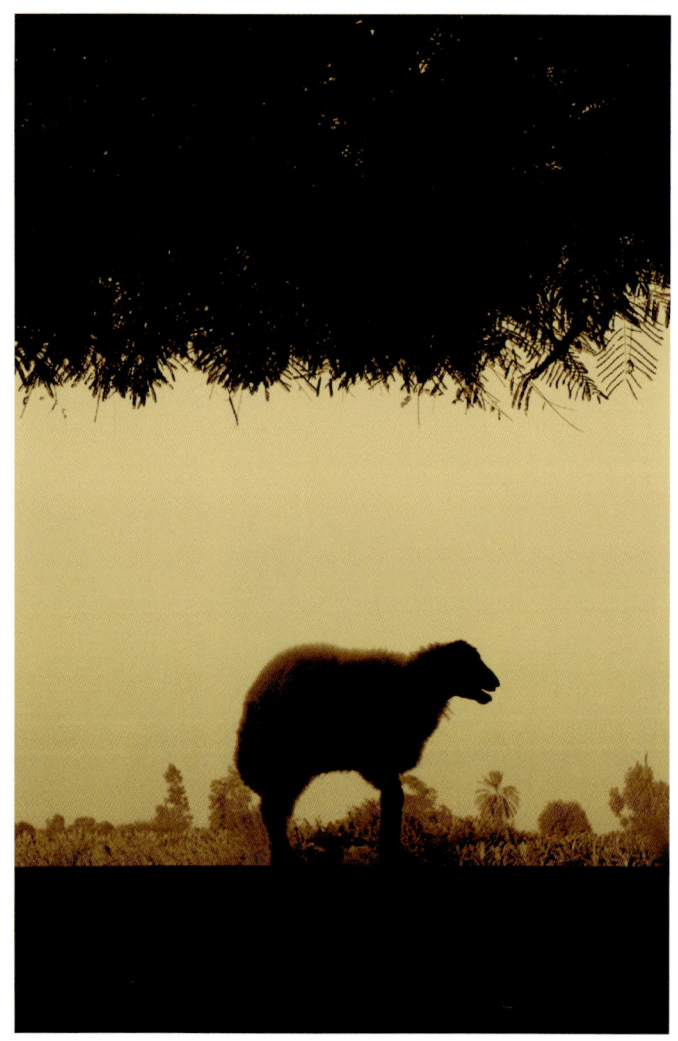

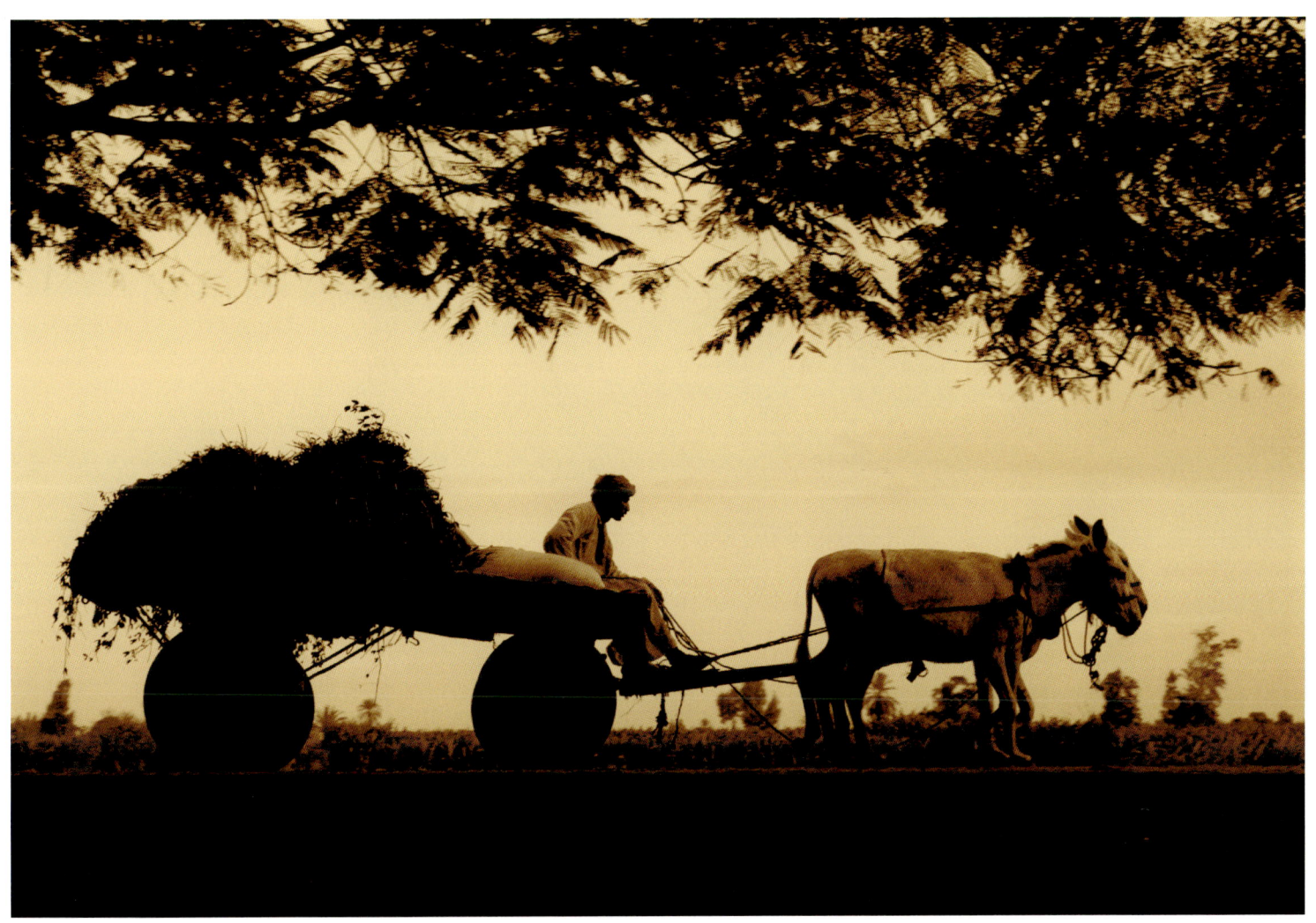

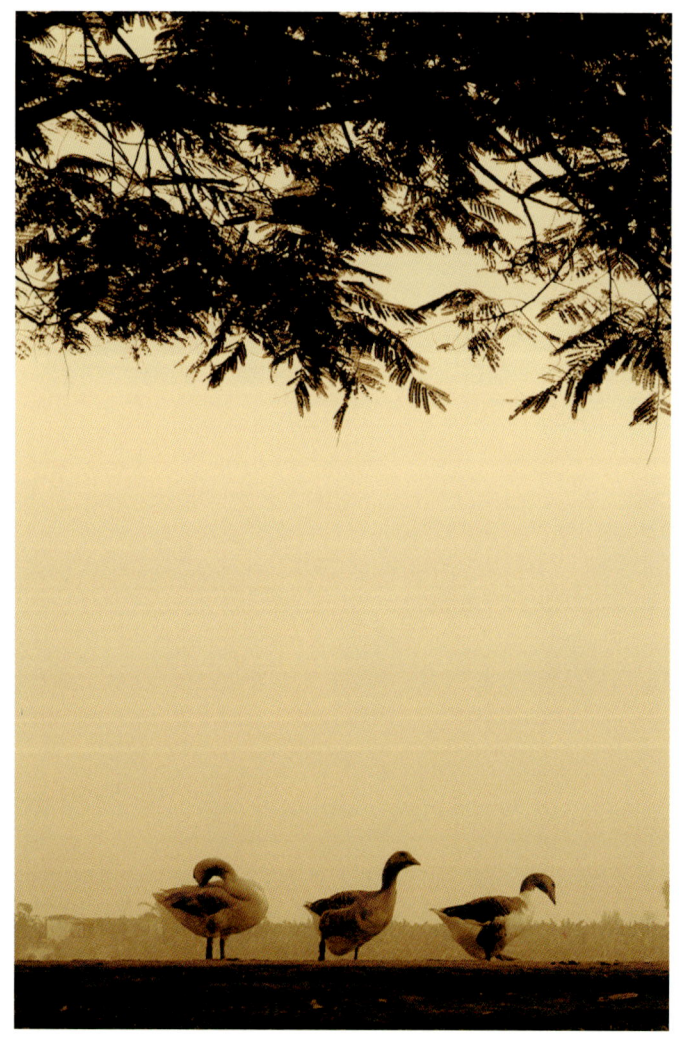

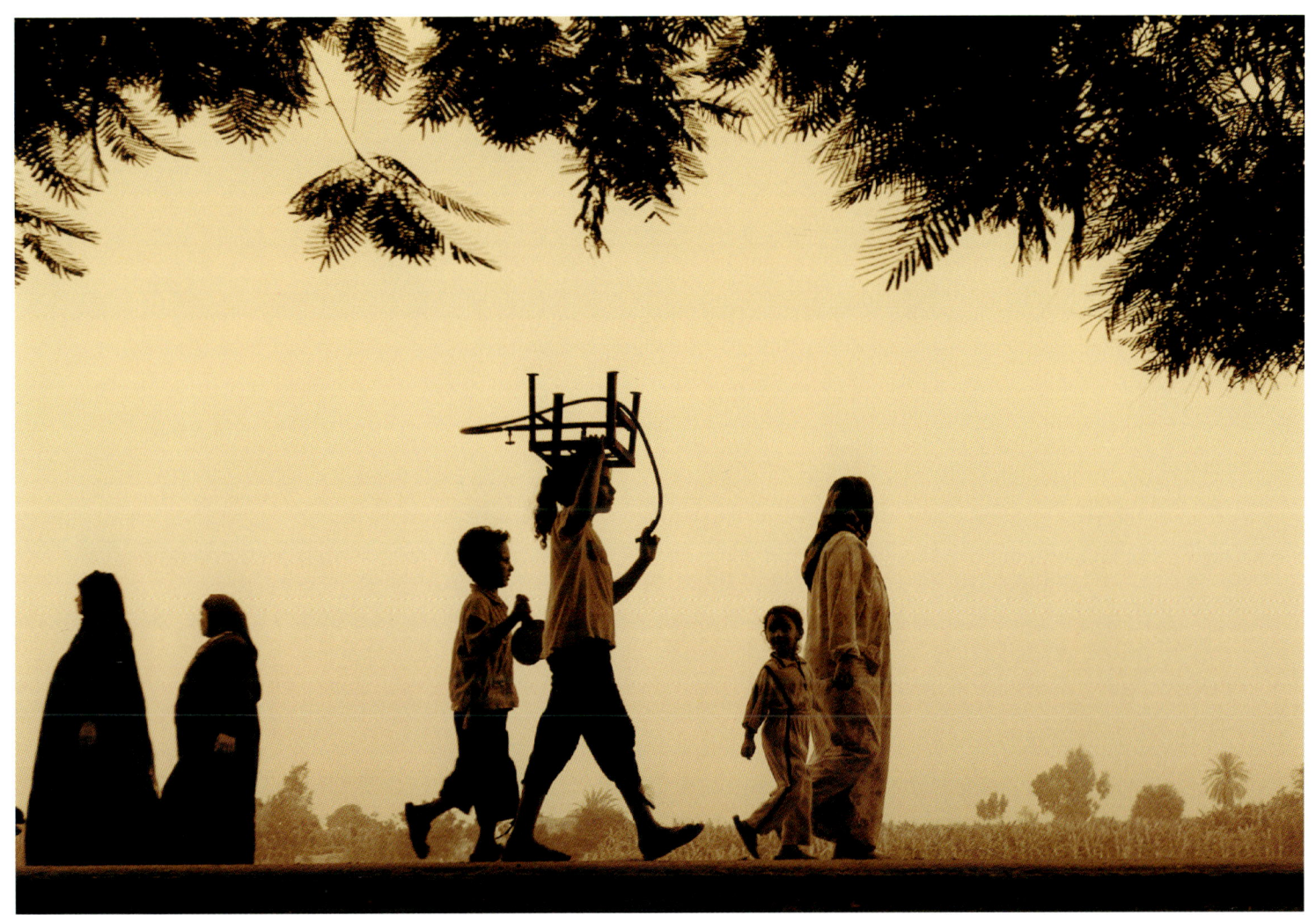

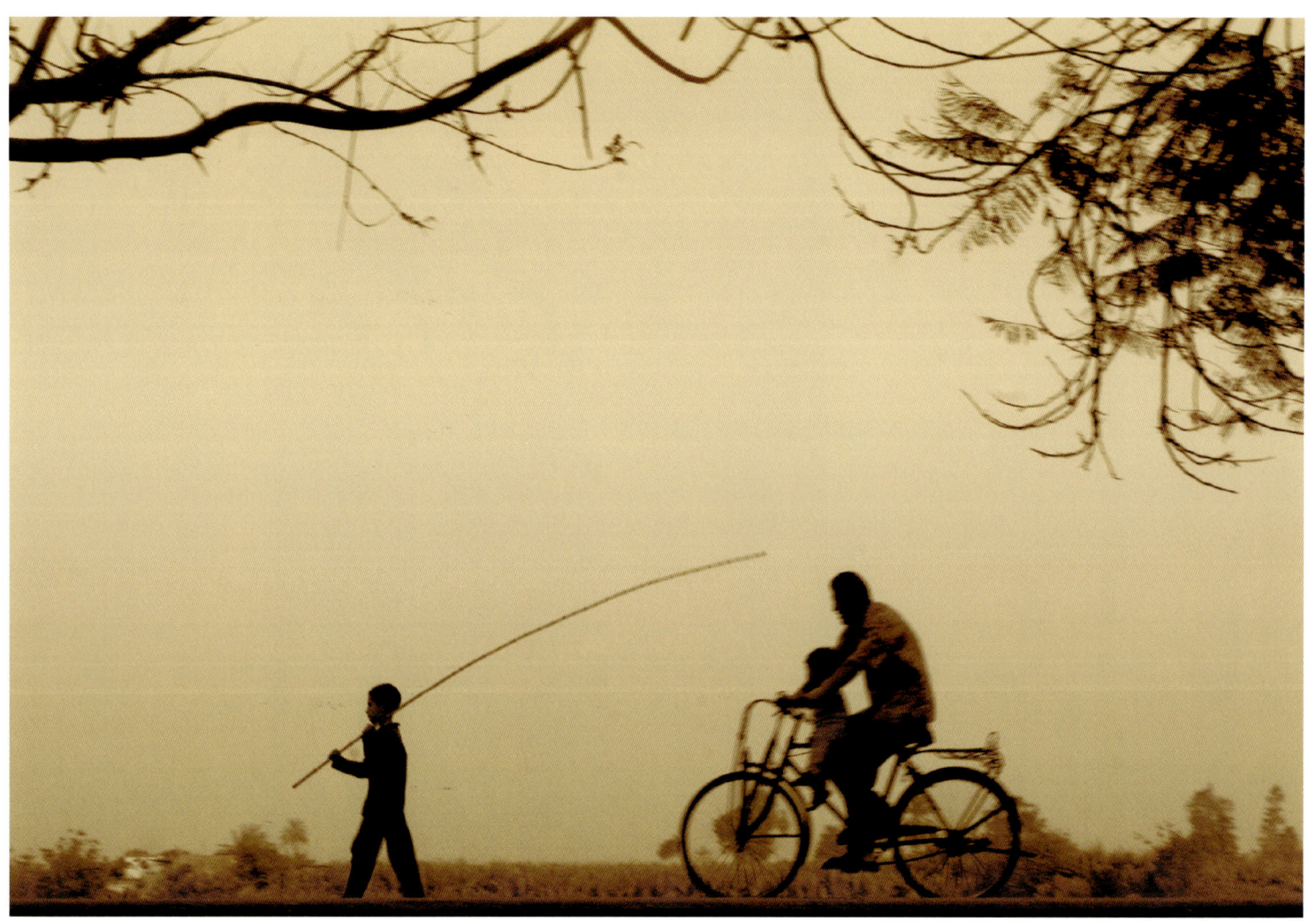

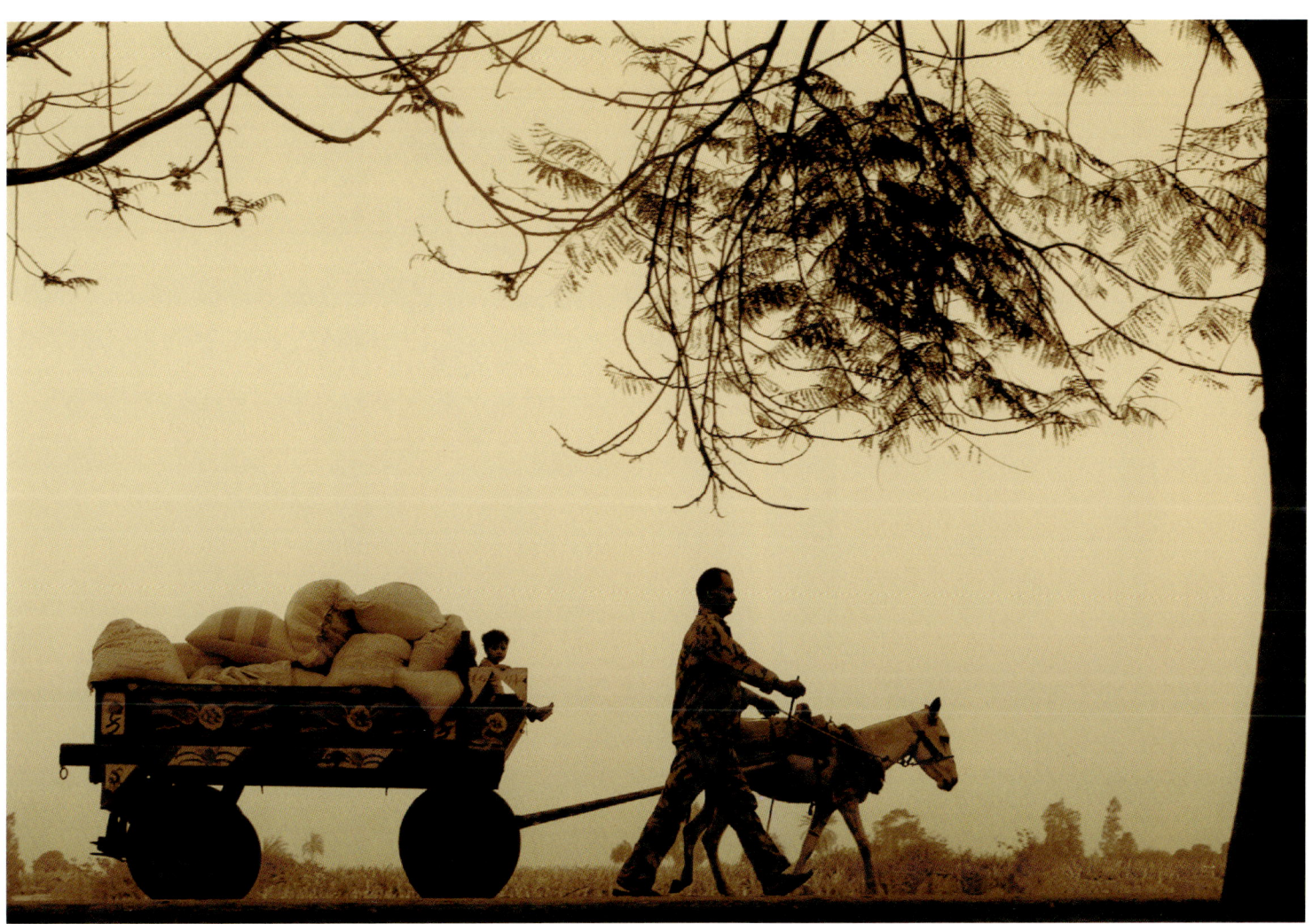

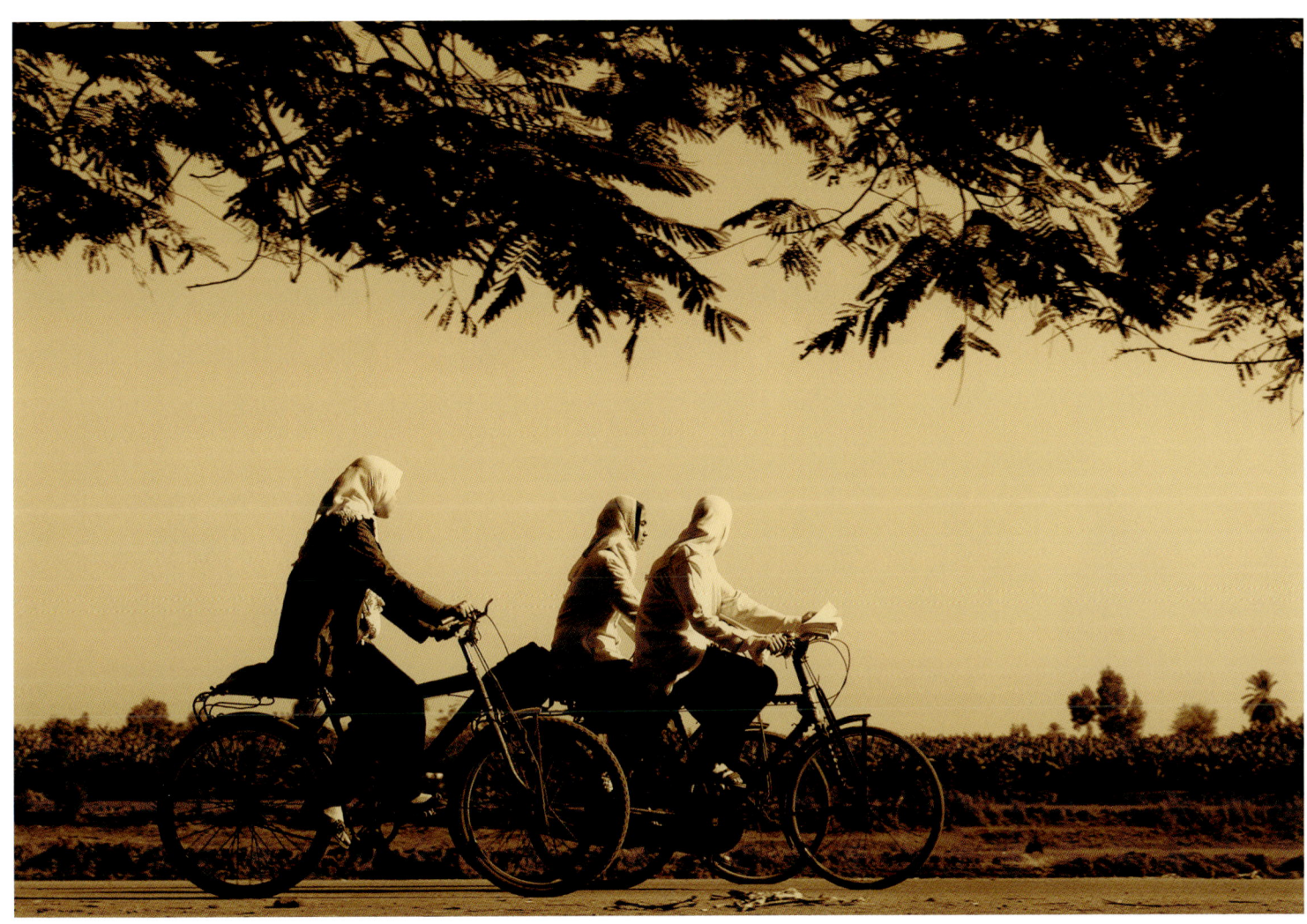

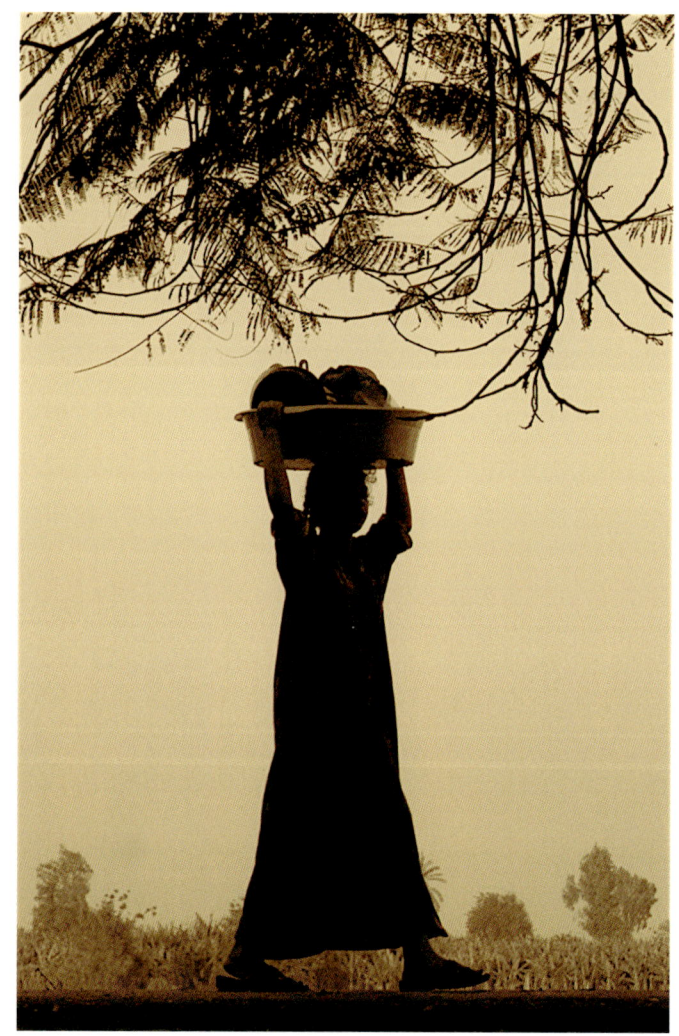

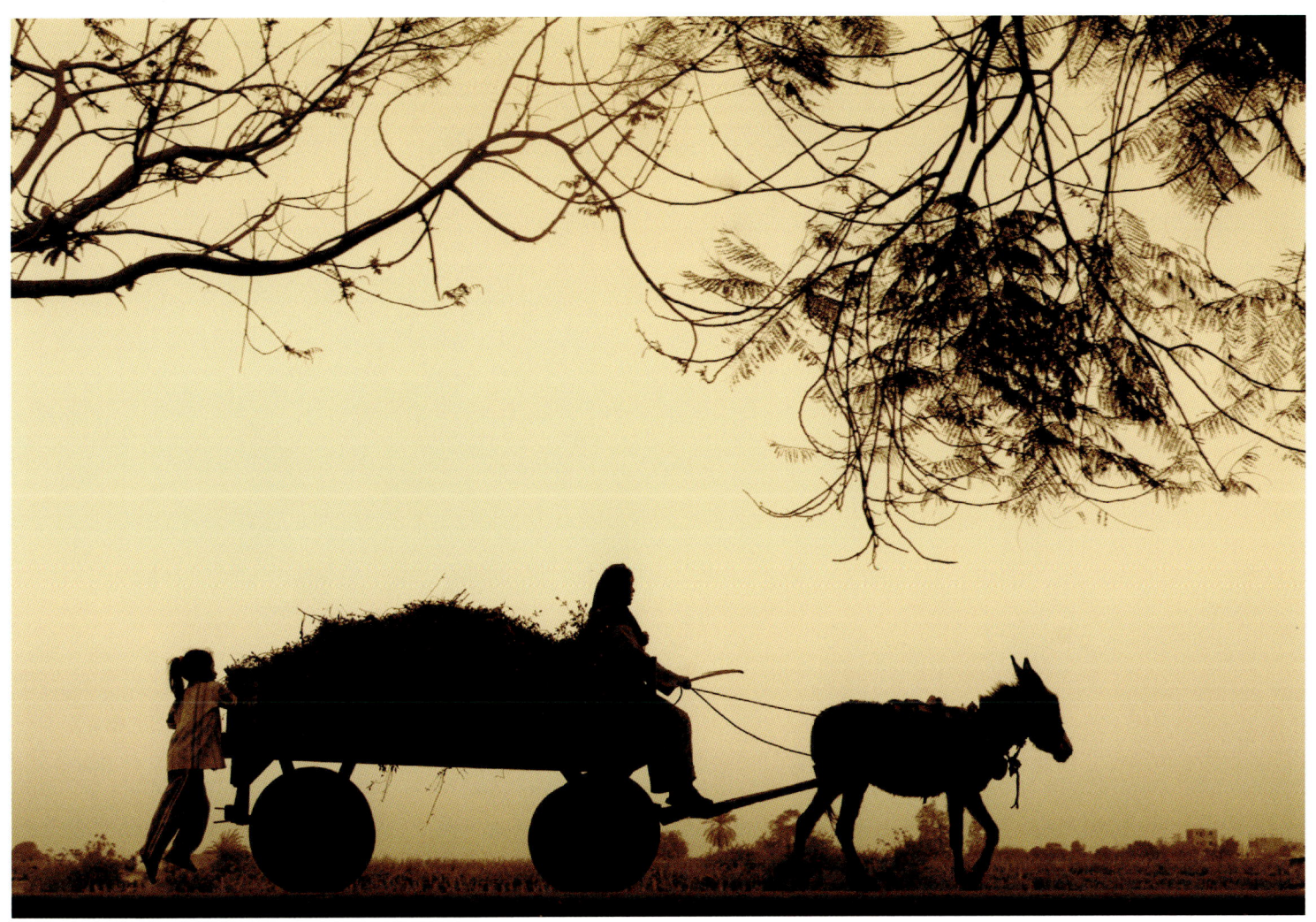

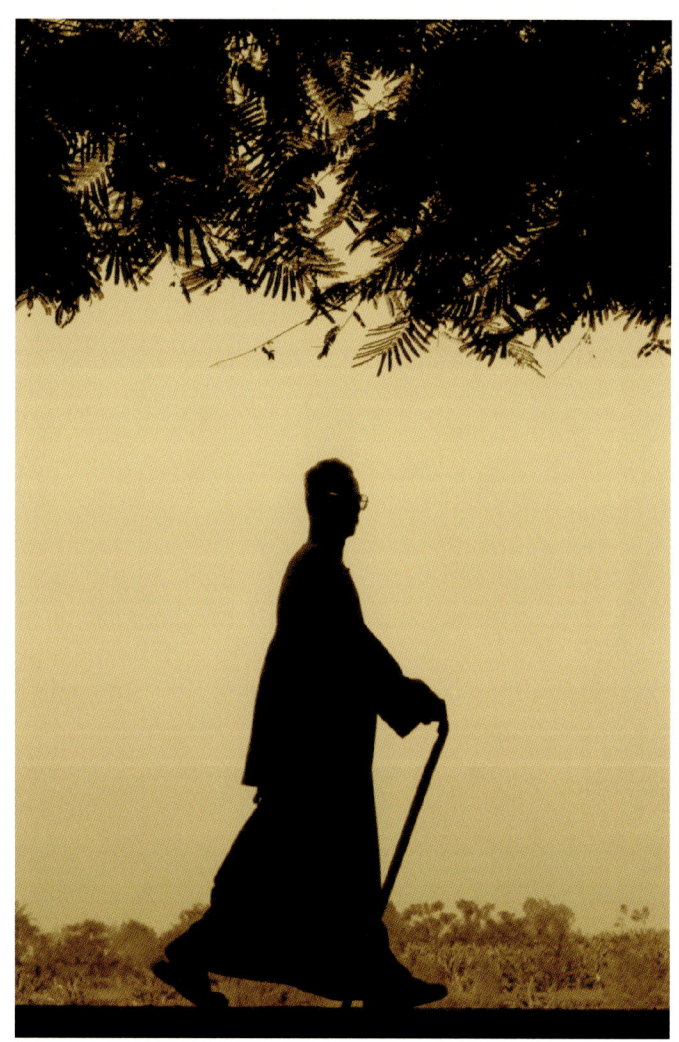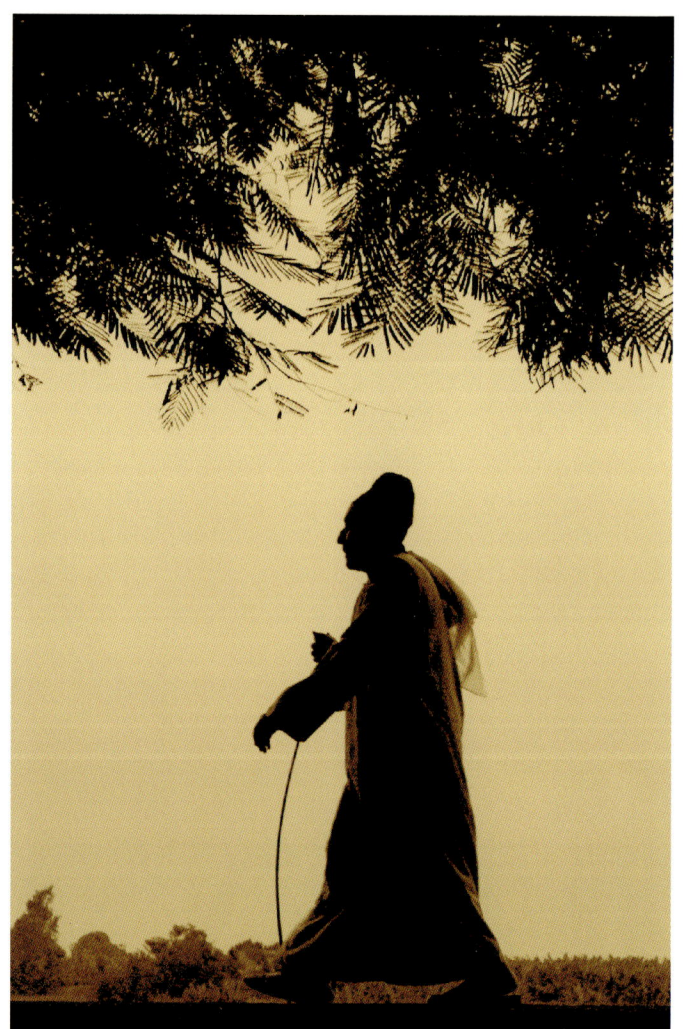

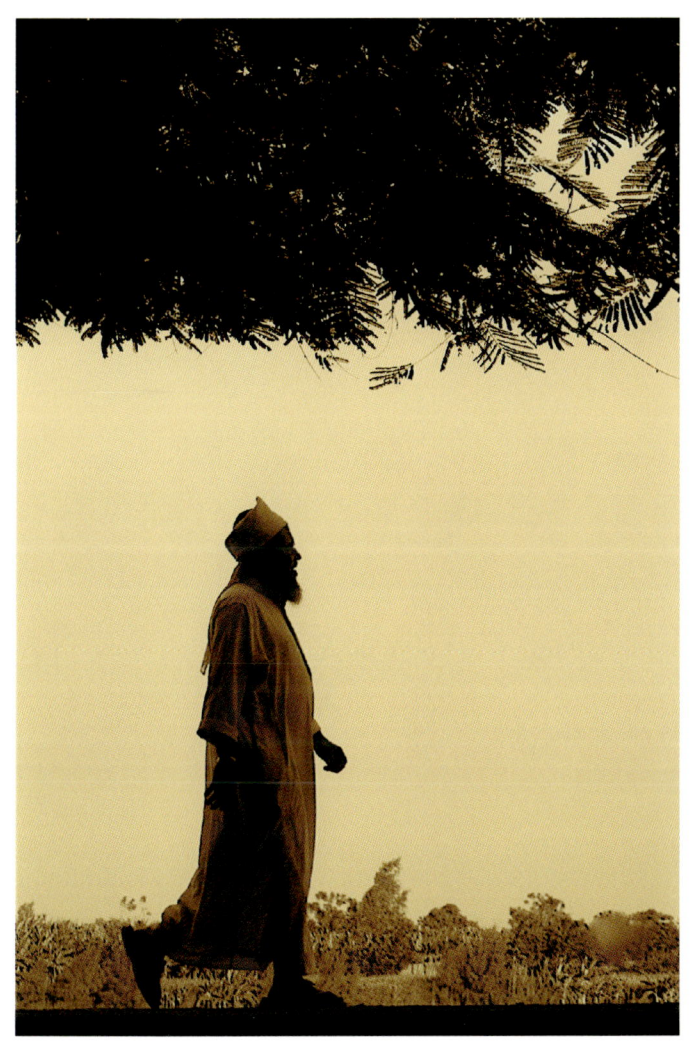
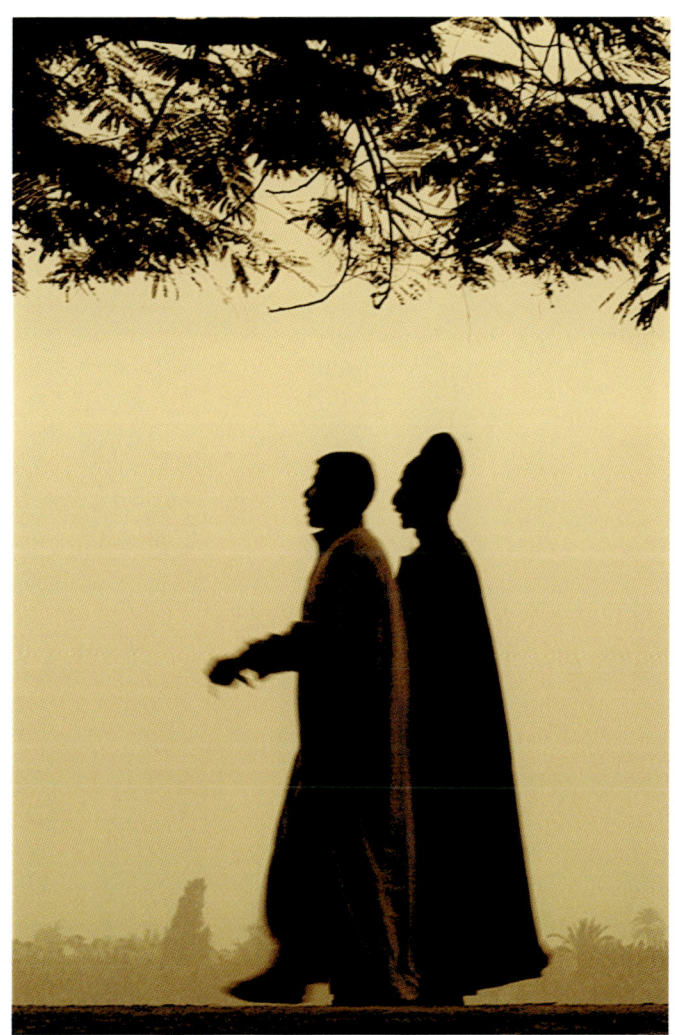

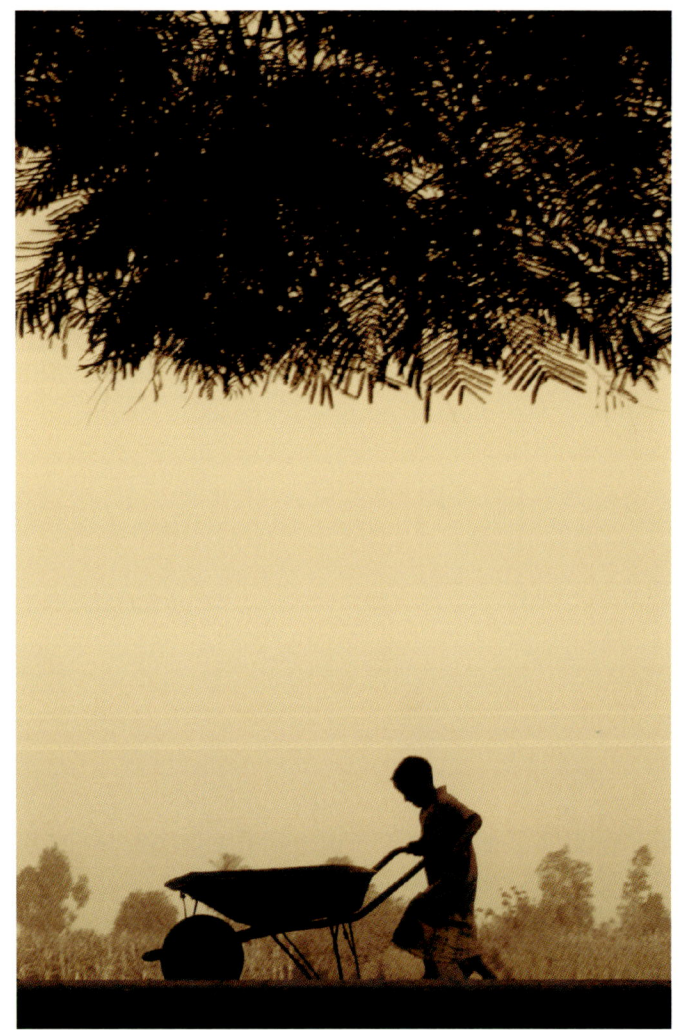

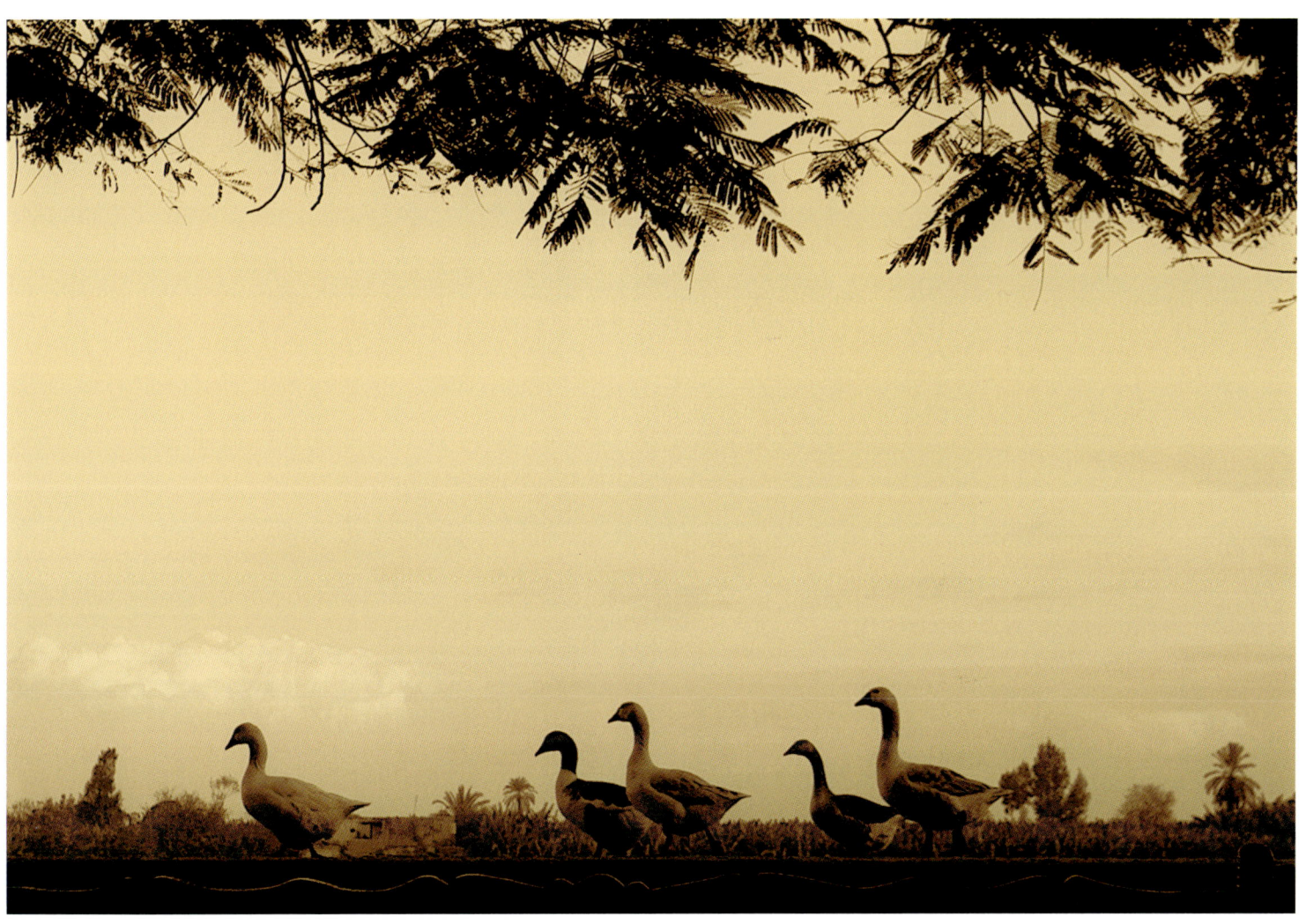

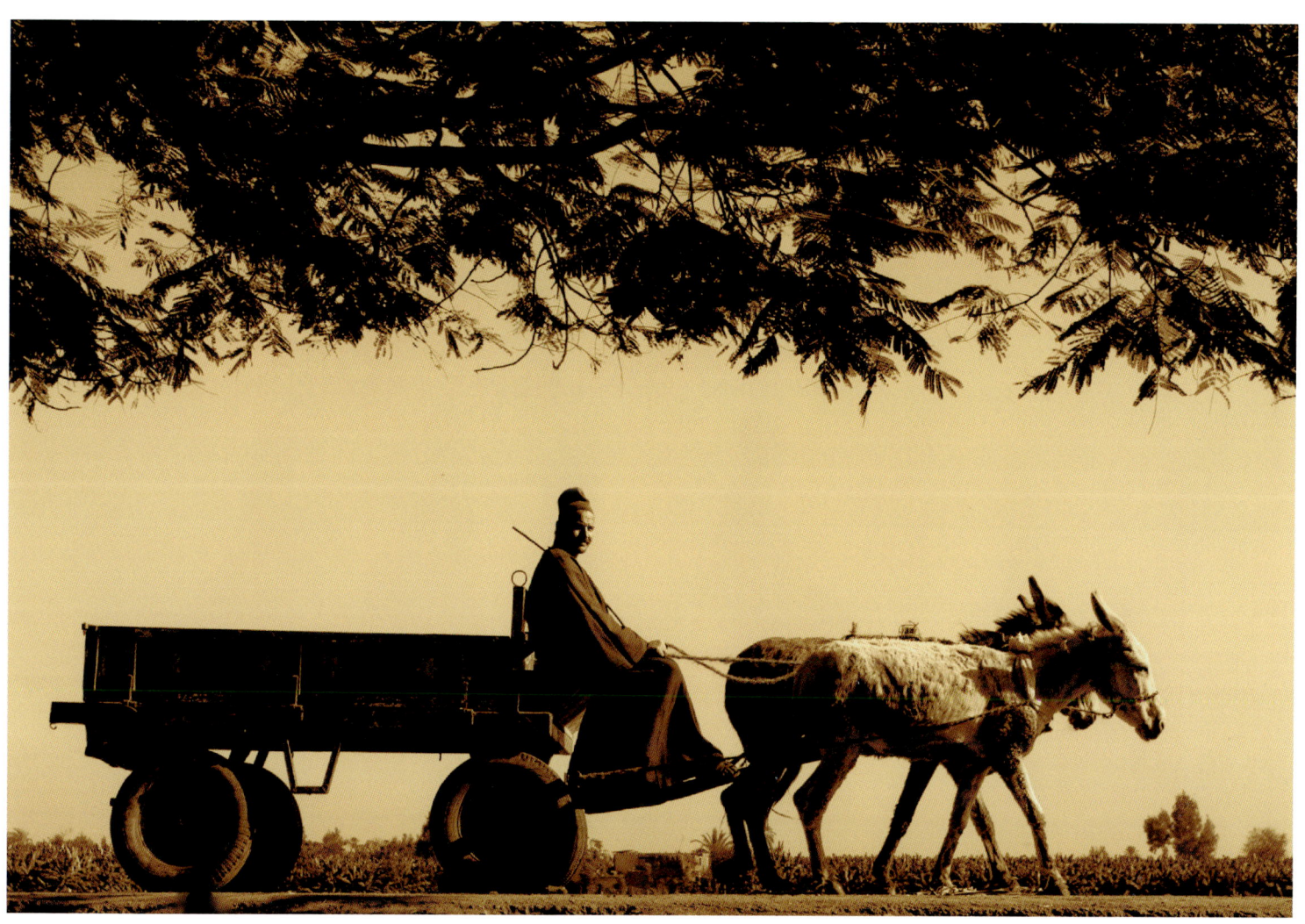

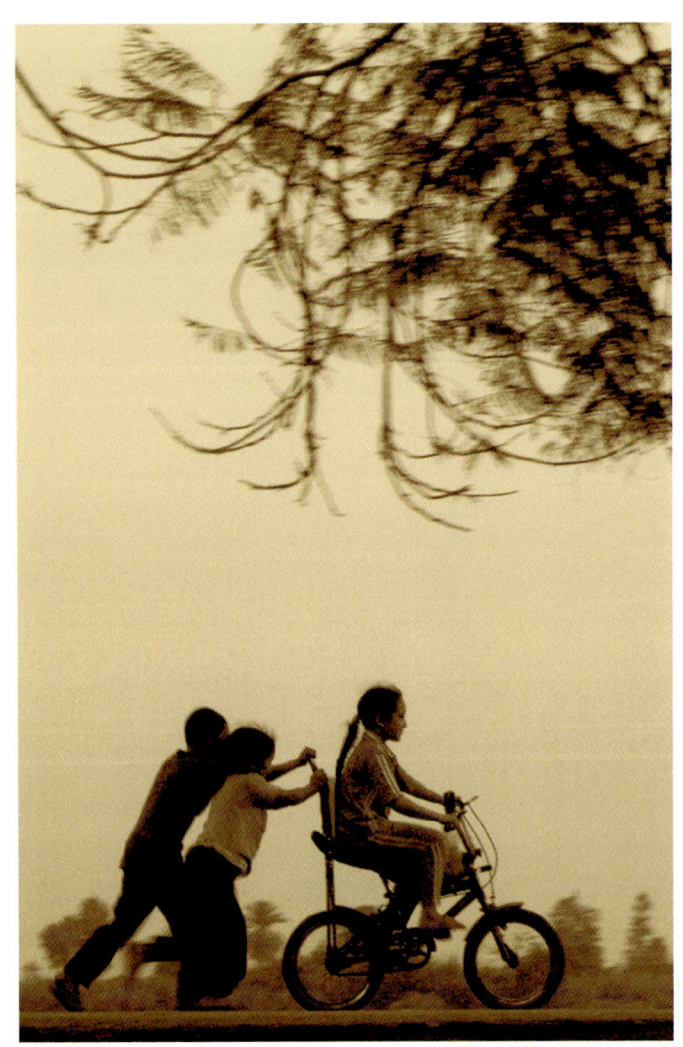

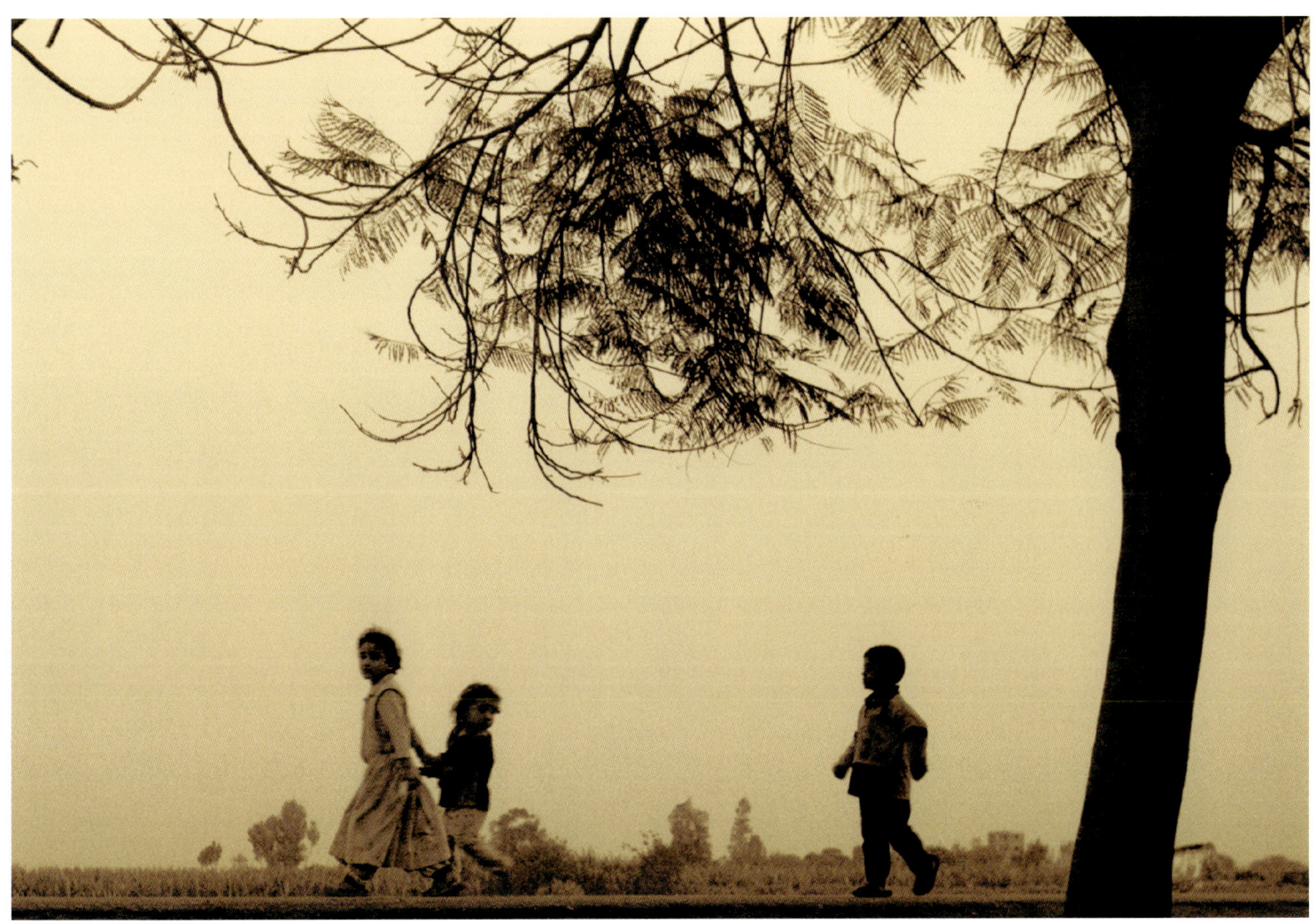

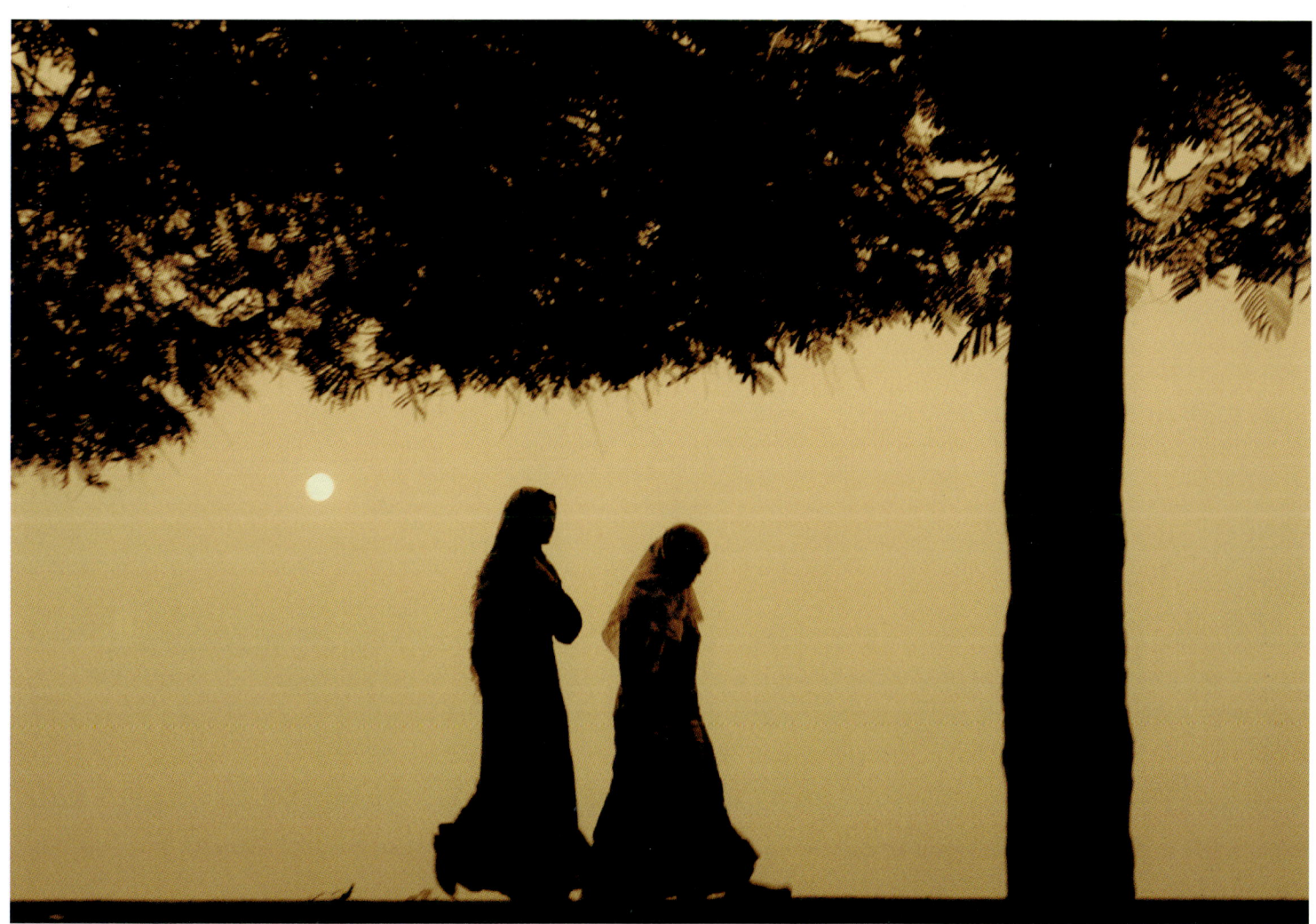

Acknowledgments

I commend all those at the American University in Cairo Press who have worked to bring this book to fruition. In particular I want to thank Mark Linz, who immediately said Yes to the project, Miriam Fahmi for her knowledge of production matters and caring attention to detail, and Andrea El-Akshar who respected my sequencing of images and gave the book the right graphic mood. A special thanks to Neil Hewison, who had the rare talent of seeing that all the pieces fit, responded warmly to both my words and images, edited the text with insight and sensitivity, and showed me his kind and patient manner when my knowledge of technical digital matters fell short. I appreciate having the renowned poet Muhammad Afifi Matar add another dimension to the book with his revealing and moving autobiographical vignettes. I thank each and every villager who gave me the gift of their expressive forms and gestures, as well as the *omda* of the village and his family, who never failed to make me welcome to their home. I thank the many friends and colleagues who looked at the images and reinforced my belief in the project: the names of Cora Edmonds, Tony and Judy King, Ruth and David Noble, Mary Louise Pierson, Ute Stebich, Lise and August Uribe, and Joan Wortis especially come to mind. I am also grateful to Brian Crowley, who stepped in when needed with his impressive knowledge of digital imaging. Finally, I thank my husband, Hamdi Abdel Shaheed Lasheen, who sat with me on every visit to the *omda*'s house, became my extra pair of eyes, never pushed me to leave before I felt ready, and slowly deepened my understanding of village ways with his careful explanations. I dedicate this book to him.